mɪɴᴅfuʟɴᴇss

for everyday living

mindfulness

for everyday living

CHRISTOPHER TITMUSS

BARRON'S

First edition for the United States and Canada
published in 2003 by Barron's Educational Series, Inc.

First published in 2002 under the title *Mindfulness for Everyday Living*
by Godsfield Press, Laurel House, Station Approach, Alresford,
Hants, SO24 9JH, United Kingdom.

Designed and created by The Bridgewater Book Company

All inquiries should be addressed to:
Barron's Educational Series, Inc.
250 Wireless Boulevard
Hauppauge, New York 11788

http://www.barronseduc.com

International Standard Book Number 0-7641-2260-6

Library of Congress Catalog Card Number 2001099144

Printed in China

9 8 7 6 5 4 3 2 1

contents

preface

In my early twenties I hitchhiked to India, where I first became exposed to the Buddhist tradition with its emphasis on mindfulness, non-clinging, compassion, and liberation. In 1970 I took ordination as a Buddhist monk in Thailand to develop the range of spiritual practices and deep meditation offered in the tradition. After six years as a monk, I disrobed and then returned to the West. These teachings and practices have as much relevance in Western society as in a monastery in the East.

We can all live free, contented, and intelligent lives if we are willing to take a genuine and deep interest in our daily activities. Whatever your spiritual persuasion and level of experience, you should find *Mindfulness for Everyday Living* an inspiring and practical guide to facing daily challenges, such as fostering creativity, understanding your relationship to daily life, and dealing with physical and emotional pain. Discover how mindfulness can put you more closely in touch with your senses, thoughts, and feelings, and can help you cope with anxiety about the unknown. My aim is to make the profound Buddhist teachings and practices on mindfulness accessible and relevant to everyone by using everyday examples and simple exercises.

Time and time again we find ourselves making mistakes, acting in confused ways, or driving ourselves too hard because we are not mindful of what we are doing. Drawing on my own personal experience and the timeless insights of the Buddhist tradition, I show how making a conscious and careful commitment to mindfulness can open your eyes to a new appreciation of life in this remarkable world.

Mindfulness for Everyday Living examines major issues of our daily life from infatuation with goods, monitoring of our energy, sexual relationships, health, making changes in our lives, loneliness, friendship, meditation and living with wisdom, provoking thought, and a shift in experience in our inner life. Our society often takes the view that we must engage ourselves in more and more doing. Mindfulness gives a priority instead to a way to being in the world with full presence and total interest.

I believe that this book comes at a time when institutions, whether business, health, or religious, show more and more interest in the power of mindfulness to change people's lives, whether employees, patients, or spiritual practitioners. Originally confined to Buddhist monasteries of Southeast Asia, the practice of mindfulness has a daily relevance for calmness, insight, and profound transformation. I strongly believe that if the principles and practices of mindfulness become widespread, from primary schools to the upper echelons of business, it will mark a profound change in direction and values of society. Coupled with specific meditation practice, the application of mindfulness may well come to be regarded as a major turning point in Western society from being consumer driven to living with mindfulness, respect, and deep concern for our interdependence with the world. I hope it will help to point the way forward, providing an invaluable resource for daily life. The smallest spark can light a great fire for change.

INTRODUCTION:

The Power of Living Mindfully

Mindfulness is an indispensable tool for daily living. It helps us to cultivate a clear and comprehensive awareness of what is happening while it is happening without allowing the mind to wander. Living mindfully, we develop a fresh relationship to all of our everyday activities, from brushing our teeth, to engaging in work, to making love. Practicing mindfulness awakens us to a liberated life and the experience of natural joy day to day. It keeps us connected to the world around us and to ourselves. Through the power of mindfulness, we recognize that the here and now can be a vehicle leading to profound understanding.

We often don't realize how unmindful and out of touch we have become. We race out of the house in the morning to make an appointment, forgetting to take with us the necessary papers. Daydreaming while driving the car, we find ourselves slamming on the brakes to avoid smashing into the car in front. Eating unmindfully, we eat the wrong things or wind up feeling guilty for slouching on the sofa watching television while polishing off a large bag of potato chips. We forget to send a get well card to a friend who is seriously ill. We put something away for safekeeping, but we can't remember where we put it. Unmindful of what we say or write, we hurt someone's

feelings and lose a friend. We allow ourselves to dwell on the past or the future or to worry excessively about a problem, unmindful of the pressure we build up inside.

The practice of mindfulness changes our relationship to daily life so that we feel more in tune with ourselves, with others, and with what is happening around us. When we let go of daydreams, fantasies, mental wandering, and excessive thinking, we don't make foolish mistakes, become forgetful, and cause problems for ourselves and others. Instead, we deepen our harmonious relationship with daily life and learn to love the challenge of working with the ordinary and the everyday.

Mindfulness has been at the heart of spiritual practice in the Buddhist tradition for over 2,500 years. Faith, love, charitable deeds, and service to others readily come to mind as expressions of the spiritual life, but living mindfully is as profound a spiritual practice as any of these. The Buddhist tradition takes an expansive view of the significance of mindfulness. It holds that every activity, no matter how trivial or familiar, is worthy of full attention. In the light of mindfulness, everything matters equally. All activities fit into the scheme of things, into the web of existence, and therefore deserve our wholehearted awareness and presence.

Buddhism holds that it is important to be mindful of what we have done, what we are doing, and what we need to do. It reminds us that to live mindfully is to live wisely, so that we avoid having to keep clearing up the confusion we generate through heedless behavior. The teachings of the Buddha remind us of the importance of the living present. They emphasize that when we look directly into this present moment, we do not become lost in reactive and habitual mind states. We have all seen statues of the Buddha in the standing posture. These remind followers of the teachings of the value of a calm abiding, of moment-to-moment attention.

Yet, we do not have to have any particular religious beliefs to practice mindfulness, as we can readily experience for ourselves the enlightening impact of mindfulness on daily existence. If we commit ourselves to the practice of heedful living, we experience countless benefits. We develop respect, care, and appreciation for our place in this world. We become calm and find it easy to concentrate. We experience the here and now in ever deepening ways. Through our developing power of observation, we see things clearly and are able to respond from that clarity.

We are also better able to cope with the frustrations of everyday life. Buses do not always run on time. Traffic jams, breakdowns, drivers who fail to turn up for work all affect the service. Complaining or becoming angry has no effect on a late bus; such reactions just work us up into a frenzy of agitation. When we are unsettled and out of touch with the present moment, our perceptions are distorted, though we often forget this. An unsettled mind blocks our ability to see things as they are. We get caught up in our imagination and sacrifice peace of mind to our demands and expectations. Rather than allowing ourselves to react in this habitual way, we can make a late bus into an opportunity to develop calmness, contentment, and patience. Like a Buddha, we can stand still. Mindful. Aware. Present.

When we abide in a stabilized and contented way with the present, we can also turn our attention to the past and see it clearly, without the projections we manufacture through agitation. When we've had an argument with a friend, we often go over and over the conversation in our minds, justifying our position and becoming more and more angry and upset. Mindfulness teaches us to listen so deeply that we can hear the feelings behind the words. It helps us to remember that maybe our friend was ill, or worried about something, or just confused, as we often are. It helps us to relax and let go.

We can also turn our attention to the future in a mindful way. My work causes me to travel a great deal. I often make arrangements with various centers and organizations around the world more than a year in advance. I try to be mindful of the details— fixing dates, looking up train and flight times, making advance bookings, securing reasonably priced tickets, and keeping handy a list of items that I need to take with me on a journey. I find that applying a mindful and systematic approach to travel takes little time, unfolds without pressure, and makes the task of traveling much easier.

Though the practice of mindfulness may sound like a rather simple undertaking, it actually challenges every cell of our being. Mindfulness practice can act as a stepping stone to deep and lasting inner change. It brings up areas of our inner life that we neglect. It causes us to ask ourselves: What do I need to develop? What do I need to let go of? What matters? What doesn't matter? What changes do I need to make in my life?

Mindfulness teaches us to walk the edge rather than to withdraw, become a submissive personality, or give in to old fears. It helps us to confront our inhibitions and gives us the strength and power of mind to face anything that arises inside ourselves or in the outside world. As we become more mindful of the consequences of what we do and what we fail to do, we learn a great deal about ourselves.

Contemporary psychotherapy often emphasizes looking into the events of the past to resolve problems that arise in the present. That approach may be useful for some people, but it is not the only way. When we develop the power of mindfulness, old problems begin to lose their grip over our lives because we don't keep dwelling on them. A woman once confided to me that she spent a lot of time thinking about her unhappy childhood. She told me that she wakes up in the morning feeling heavy and reluctant to get out of bed. "Since I can't help dwelling on the past, I don't feel any joy in the present. I seem to spend a lot of time in therapy going over the past. I'm not sure if that's the best thing for me." As we talked, we explored the possibility of her focusing on the here and now to safeguard her from indulging in memories. I assured the woman that it is possible to make profound changes to her sense of self-worth without going into the past to resolve old problems. Mindfulness is a practical therapeutic alternative. The Buddha said that he taught mindfulness to

"overcome grief, sorrow, and despair" and the "whole mass of suffering." He did not place significance on analyzing what happened in our childhood. I suggested to the woman that perhaps a combination of therapy and mindfulness training would help her to rediscover her joy in living.

We often imagine that success and happiness go together. This is often not the case, as so-called successful people often find out to their cost. However, a genuinely mindful life and happiness do go together. The more we practice, the more we realize that mindfulness is a simple and readily available resource for the young and old, the healthy and sick, the successful and unsuccessful. Each of us can benefit from mindful living and the practices that support it.

I know of one mindfulness teacher who works with people who are often extremely overweight. In one exercise, he asks his students to eat a raisin, telling them to chew the tiny dried fruit as slowly and as mindfully as possible. It is not unusual for people who participate in this exercise to report that it's the first time they have really allowed themselves to taste a raisin. By applying mindfulness to every experience of eating, many people find that they consume less food and avoid having to put themselves under the pressure of a strict diet regime.

There is really no time like the present. Mindfulness is simply a matter of intention.
- *Instead of hurrying from one thing to another, or trying to do too many things at the same time, focus on the activity at hand.*
- *Don't watch television, read a magazine, and eat at the same time, especially if you have issues around food.*
- *Can you allow the telephone to ring a couple of times before you answer it?*
- *Can you take your time to wash the dishes, prepare the vegetables, clean the car, or cut the grass so that it becomes a mindful activity rather than a task or an obligation?*

Learn to approach the obligations of your life with relaxed contentment. Life is full of tremendous trifles. Mindfulness develops the appreciation that every activity belongs to the great web of life. Trapped in our habits and conditioning, we engage in much of what we do in a preoccupied or distracted way. These patterns dull our daily lives so that we often hate doing certain things. We convince ourselves that the tasks are the problem. Yet it is our relationship to those daily responsibilities that matters.

Anything that we do regularly can become routine and cause us to resist it. Mindfulness helps break through resistance so that we experience love and connection with what we are doing, no matter how many times an action is repeated. It's easy to become trapped in the mind's worst dilemma—wanting to do one thing and not wanting to do something else. When we develop the power of mindfulness, we take the sting out of such unhealthy and imprisoning mind states. We feel less needy, less dependent on others, a greater sense of inner security, and a moment-to-moment connection and interest with what is here and now. Mindfulness practice points to calmness, deep insights into daily life, and opening of the heart and serves as a vehicle for enlightening our existence.

Let's start right now.

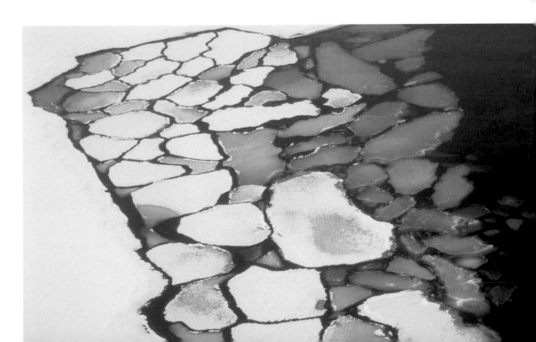

1: mindfulness of activities

breathing mindfully

Every breath we take confirms our moment-to-moment relationship with the world. The ongoing rhythm of inhalation and exhalation gives us the nourishment we need to live and eliminates the waste that would suffocate us if we could not let it go. With every in-breath, we draw in oxygen that the heart pumps through the lungs to fuel the life process in the cells of the body. With every out-breath, the cells' waste is pumped out in the form of carbon dioxide and released back into the air. This cycle of nourishment and elimination goes on throughout our life whether or not we are mindful of it.

Think about it! There is something quite extraordinary about this whole process of organic life interacting moment by moment with the environment. Moreover, no two breaths are the same. Sometimes, we draw in a longer breath due to physical exertion, physical pain, intention, or emotional upheaval. Breathing deeply, whether through exercise or intention, is important for the body, since full breaths nourish the cells more completely. People who do not engage regularly in activities that encourage deep breathing risk negative consequences to their physical health. All cells need enlivening regularly through deep breathing, whether the body is moving or still.

At other times, we draw in only a little air, because of fear, habit, or meditative calmness. Practitioners of meditation know that when we are in a state of inner serenity and stillness the body seems to need little air to circulate through the cells, yet the vibrations of the whole body can be experienced. When we sit with a straight back in an upright posture, every part of the body can relax and expand, rather than being tense and under pressure. Though the body requires little air, the oxygen we do inhale circulates freely. When we sit calmly and bring mindfulness to the breath, we flood the body with life energy from head to toe. Sometimes, we seem to experience the whole body breathing, even when inhaling only a little air.

We take so many things for granted, including the breath. We hardly pay attention to it except when we are having difficulty catching it due to exertion or illness. Then we notice the impact of the breath because it is different from our normal pattern of respiration. During a visit to Israel, a teacher of meditation gave instructions on mindfulness of breathing to a sixty-year-old grandmother. She sat with her back straight and consciously breathed in and out, allowing the breath to penetrate deep into her lungs. After a single mindful breath, she burst into tears. "I've been alive for six decades, and this is the first time that I've ever experienced myself breathing," she said.

Mindfulness of breathing is a wonderful resource. Setting aside even a few minutes every day to breathe with awareness can contribute so much to our emotional, mental, and spiritual well-being. Specifically, mindfulness of breathing helps us to achieve:

- *calmness and concentration*
- *the feeling of being centered*
- *harmony of body and mind*
- *the ability to stay steady in stressful or threatening situations*
- *deep joy and inner contentment*
- *the capacity to clear the mind of excessive thinking*
- *a deep sense of intimacy and connection with organic life*
- *an experience of inner freedom in the midst of unfolding events*

The practice of mindfulness of breathing might be described as a spiritual science that gives us the opportunity to examine, investigate, and apply a clear awareness to the problems and frustrations of daily life. For this reason, it is the root practice in many Buddhist traditions. Breathing with awareness helps us to become increasingly conscious of our feelings, emotions, thoughts, perceptions, senses, and physical life. We learn to notice how our breath affects our state of mind and body, and how our state of mind and body affects our breath. It is not surprising, then, that the Buddha referred to mindfulness of breathing as the best of practices.

As we mindfully breathe in and out, even for a few minutes, we have the chance to relax and to cut through much that is false within—projections, daydreams, fantasies, mind games, and mental wanderings. As we gain the ability to see through our illusions, we discover for ourselves what is valid, true, and relevant. The deep task of mindfulness practice is to dissolve delusions and reveal what is real and trustworthy.

Since the breath is always with us, always valid and relevant to our lives, focusing on it helps to teach us to distinguish between truth and illusion, clarity and confusion, valid perception and illusory projection. As we grow in this skill, we find it easier to avoid conflict and inner turmoil, as well as the problems we cause for others when we confuse fact and fantasy. As we develop mindfulness of breathing, we settle into the present until we feel at home with what is.

Mindfulness is like a mirror that shows only what is in front of it. As we become more aware, we take greater interest in what the mirror reveals. With this clarity, we see what we need to develop and what we need to overcome. We might use mindfulness of breathing to practice being in the here and now. Or, we might use it to cultivate positive qualities, such as deep friendship or generosity. Mindfulness of breathing gives us the space to observe with honesty any unhealthy patterns.

PRACTICE: FOCUSING ON THE BREATH

There are several techniques for focusing on the breath. You might choose to observe the breath by focusing your attention on the spot above your upper lip where the air enters or leaves through your nostrils. Or, you can observe the rise and fall of the chest, or the rise and fall of the abdomen, during the cycle of each inhalation and exhalation. Alternatively, you can try to be aware of the whole process of the breath from start to finish. If you are just getting started with a mindfulness of breathing practice, I suggest that you try to be aware of the whole breath from the time the air travels up through your nose and down into your lungs to the final exhalation. Notice as well that the next breath may come into your body immediately after the end of the exhalation or some moments later.

EXERCISES: BREATHING MINDFULLY

• When the mind feels troubled, breathe in and breathe out deeply. You can do this breathing practice anywhere—for example walking outdoors or sitting at home. Pay particular attention to, and relax into, the out-breath.

• Make the breath a little longer and deeper than usual for the first two or three minutes so that you can experience the expansion of your body as the oxygen enters and the settling down as your body expels the carbon dioxide. Try to experience as many breaths as possible during this period. Remember that the mind most easily wanders on the out-breath. Your eyes can be open or closed.

• If you feel yourself holding back unnecessarily from a situation, then take a few breaths to breathe through any fear and then act.

• If somebody is saying unkind words to you, mindfully breathe in and out rather than react. Don't give others authority over your state of mind.

• The next time you are seated for 15 or 20 minutes, rather than reading a newspaper or watching television, give the time to mindfulness of breathing.

At the beginning, you can make the breath a little longer and deeper as you learn to pay attention. Remember, you do not think about the breath, but only observe or pay attention to the breath as it comes and goes. This practice sounds easy, but it is not. If you can stay present initially with three or four consecutive breaths, you are doing well. We often want to keep control over the breath. The mind wanders. We get bored. We get distracted. Many things can keep us from mindfulness of breathing. It is important to remember that mindfulness requires practice. We are developing the capacity to stay with the full experience of the in-breath and the full experience of the out-breath. As we cultivate greater mindfulness of breathing, we begin to experience its many benefits.

EXERCISE: CULTIVATING CALMNESS

• Put this book down, and place your hands in your lap. One hand rests of top of the other with the tips of the two thumbs touching each other.
• Make sure that your back is straight and that you are sitting comfortably. Relax into this position, breathing in and out deeply.
• Hold this position for five minutes, keeping your body as calm as possible.
• Direct your mindfulness to the sensations in your hands. Notice whether they are tense or relaxed, warm or cool, dry or moist.
• Practice this technique daily, and appreciate the calmness and freedom mindfulness of the hands gives you from the unnecessary demands you place on yourself and the world.

USING OUR HANDS AND feet

Our Hands

Many people sense the limitations of traditional values and seek fresh directions to give more meaning to life, but most would consider the step I took thirty years ago to be an extreme reaction. My dissatisfaction with conventional society led me to become a Buddhist monk. I am grateful today that I have the opportunity to pass on to others what I learned from that experience.

The year was 1970. After three years spent hitchhiking and traveling through Europe and Southern Asia, I received ordination in a remote Buddhist monastery, 15 hours by train south of Bangkok, Thailand. My first retreat lasted three years and three months. Since I did not know the Thai language, I relied on a translator when I needed to speak to the abbot, who was also my Vipassana (insight meditation) teacher.

During this long retreat, my teacher, Venerable Ajahn Dhammadharo, placed much emphasis on mindfulness of the hands. As we sat in a cross-legged position, we slowly raised one hand, with fingers outstretched, to the level of the shoulder, and then slowly returned the hand to the lap. We repeated this methodical movement frequently as a meditation exercise. The movements would have looked strange to an observer, even to monks and nuns from other meditative traditions.

As we practiced this exercise on a daily basis, I began to realize its profound significance. Many states of mind that begin deep within us find expression through the hands. Feelings of love journey out through the hands into forms of touch; angry feelings make the same

journey, showing themselves in
a clenched fist or even the pull of
a trigger. Acts of generosity travel
through the hands as well, revealing
themselves as gifts, as the hands write
out a check for a donation or simply
open wide in a generous gesture.
Alternatively, the hands can also
reveal greed, stinginess, or
manipulative intentions.

Take some time to observe mindfully
the hands of people with whom you are
speaking. Notice how the hands reveal
various states of mind—calmness and
sensitivity, or restlessness and
destructive tendencies. Practicing
mindful awareness of your own hands can also help you to cultivate a deeper and
more conscious sense of the relationship between mind and body. As I practiced
mindfulness of the hands, I came to realize the wisdom of allowing healthy and
wholesome states of mind to flow out through my hands and into beneficial
expressions of caring for people, animals, and the environment. Mindfulness of the
hands also taught me to show restraint so that I did not extend any unhealthy states
of mind out into the world.

Practicing mindfulness of the hands can reveal much about the self as well. In a way,
the hands are an extension of our inner life. What happens to the hands in a given
moment reveals much about our state of mind. When we feel nervous or unsettled,
the vibrations of this state are often revealed through the fingers tapping on the
knee, or by the repeated clasping and unclasping of the fist. Mind and body are so
intimately connected that our hand movements often serve as a public advertisement
for what is taking place in our mind.

PRACTICE: CULTIVATING MINDFULNESS OF THE HANDS

How can we cultivate mindfulness of the hands in everyday life? The following simple exercise will help to focus the mind, keep mind and body together, bring a quality of attention to each moment, and enable us to renew our whole sense of being.

Most people would feel far too self-conscious to sit with a straight back while riding the train during rush hour and practice moving the hand up and down through the air. Yet, we can practice mindfulness on the train by sitting with our hands in our lap, in probably the most famous of all *mudras* (hand positions), one hand resting on top of the other, with the ends of the thumbs just touching (see page 19). This mudra can be seen in countless Buddha images. We can imitate the Buddha's posture, even while riding the train. Sit with your hips pushed gently forward to make sure your back is in a straight and upright position. Place one hand on the top of the other with the tips of both thumbs touching each other lightly. This mudra is an invaluable resource for quietly focusing the mind. Turn the attention to the bare sensation of the contact between the tips of the two thumbs touching each other. When your mind wanders, bring it straight back to that contact. Develop a calm focus on the sensations for several minutes or longer.

PRACTICE: ACHIEVING STILLNESS

If you habitually feel tired or stressed out, pay attention to the energy you waste through scratching, fidgeting, changing position, crossing and uncrossing your legs, or fiddling around with a pen or paper clip, an item of clothing, or a strand of hair. To live a mindful life, consider the different ways that you expend energy through excess movement and restlessness. Practice being calm and still instead. Sit in the meditation mudra described in the exercise above, and you will find that you can conserve the energy of the mind and body so that it can be used for purposes that are more important.

Our Feet

To live mindfully, we need to bring full attention to the way we use our feet. We often think that our home is where we live, or where our heart is. In spiritual practice, our home is where our feet are. Where are your feet right now? Do you have both feet firmly on the ground or is one foot on the floor and the other crossed over your leg, hanging in the air? Right now feel the contact of both feet on the floor. What does that feel like?

PRACTICES: WALKING AND STANDING MINDFULLY

Buddhist practice gives more emphasis to mindful and meditative walking than to attending religious services or engaging in acts of devotion. To walk slowly and mindfully up and down, with the heels of one foot barely going in front of the toes of the other foot, is a prayer to life, an ongoing expression of devotion to each moment. We do not need to walk a great distance—the length of a room at home is long enough. The entire body should be straight and upright, particularly the head, so that the eyes look forward rather than downward. We then experience each step touching the ground and the movement of the energy as the foot slowly moves through the air to place the foot on the ground. There is the bare moment-to-moment experience of the foot making contact with the ground. We can practice this anywhere.

We can also practice standing meditation. Keep the feet a little apart, and focus your attention on the feet's contact with the ground. Keep the whole body straight, upright, with eyes closed or open. Experience the sense of your whole being.

It is easy to spend far too much time in our heads, amid a whirl of circulating ideas, plans, analysis, intellectual games, and constant commentary, and we often lose access to much of the rest of the body. We need to practice mindfulness of the feet as a vehicle for insight and understanding about ourselves. There are many examples of this. If we rush to get from A to B, what is our state of mind? If we wander around, up and down, rather aimlessly, what is going on within? If we walk in a fast, intense way, what does it tell us? There is a link between feet and mind that can provide us with the opportunity for insight. However we are walking, we can bring mindfulness to our activity by stopping for a moment and focusing. We can then continue our journey, but with a mindful and calm attitude.

We can also engage in deep reflection while walking that can shake us out of complacency in terms of the way we relate to the experience of walking. We have become so habitualized that we take walking for granted. We never question the act of walking, or contemplate the walker who appears to accompany the walking. There is a precious quality to walking meditation that offers an opportunity for liberating insights into the mystery of this moment-to-moment unfolding.

EXERCISE: EXPERIENCING MINDFUL MOVEMENT
Sit with your back straight with your right hand (if you are right-handed) on top of your leg. Very slowly, lift up your hand and moment by moment experience moving it through the air. Practice slowly and mindfully reaching out to any small object in front of you. Pick it up slowly and feel the sensation of holding it. Then stretch your arm out again and put the object in your hand back where it came from. Keep practicing for several minutes to make the connection between mindfulness and movement of your hand.

CReatiNG aNd DISSOLViNG

Creating

There are many extraordinary ways to express creativity through the body, whether it is through the harmonious movement of Tai Chi, the subtle postures of yoga, the refined extension of the limbs in ballet, or the power of contemporary dance. No matter what our age, we can all make opportunities for creative expression. Music has the power to transform our inner life, as well as give us much pleasure and enjoyment. Movement and music mutually support each other, from the tapping of the fingers to a dance in which we respond with every cell in our body.

We can select pieces of music that express our different moods, then learn to move our body in different ways in harmony with the music. The following are four different moods of music that touch deep places in our inner life.

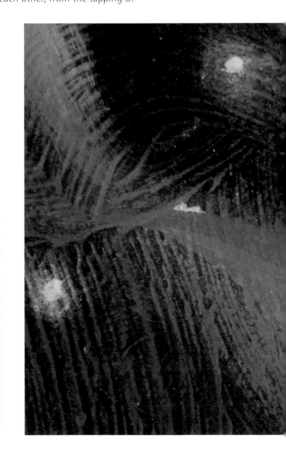

1 MUSIC FOR INNER PEACE
This music brings a sublime sense of inner peace and calm, encouraging us to dance lovingly, gently, and peacefully in harmony with the rhythm of the music. Gently the body sways and unfolds itself from one moment to the next, capturing the lucid tones from the loudspeaker so the music and the body harmonize. Such music has the power to touch places of love and contentment deep inside our being.

2 MUSIC TO TRANSFORM ENERGY

At times, we may experience waves of positive or negative energy. We need to let that energy flow throughout our whole being, rather than allow it to remain stuck, leaving us highly excited and potentially explosive. For example, we may feel uptight or angry about something. Our angry words can have  a destructive impact upon another person. When this negative energy impacts on our consciousness, instead of getting angry, we can put on energizing music and let our body dance, moving deliberately all the way from head to toes. Loud and upbeat, this music corresponds to our mood. Vibrant music can help transform our anger into a sense of oneness. If we move and gyrate our arms, legs, and trunk of the body in all directions, our energy can flow freely.

3 MUSIC THAT IS SPIRITUALLY UPLIFTING

The voices of the choir, an evening raga, chanting, or the opera singer in full flow of expression can all energize a spiritual sense of life. This music has the power to reach into the heart of our consciousness, bringing us closer to God. Our movement to this type of music is a prayer to life, an offering to existence, and a gesture of devotional love for all forms of existence. Through such movement and music, we uplift the spirit and gain a sense of the sacred, here and now. We experience our home as a temple on Earth.

4 MUSIC THAT EMBRACES A VARIETY OF MOODS

From classical to New Age music, from East to West, North to South, there are forms of music that shift gear in a matter of moments or minutes to reach different places within our being. From inner peace, to dynamic expression, to spiritual uplifting, we can harmonize our body with the changing rhythms as a way to express ourselves.

By connecting with any of these four kinds of music through movement, we cultivate our capacity to express what we feel. Music from all over the world has the potential to transform our inner life, whether it is gentle, rapid, or transcendental. It is an invaluable resource for our inner well-being, enabling us to express our changing feelings and experiences. Sometimes, we can use music as a catalyst for helping to release emotions, transform them, generate energy, or burn off excess energy.

I call the practice of employing music for relaxation, insight, and transforming of energy "Dharma Dancing." I recently attended a formless dance class that encouraged us to move our bodies freely during a two-hour period. I had anticipated that there would be a break during the middle of the class, but the dance teacher continued to play the music and we, the students, continued to dance even when we felt tired or resistant. I noticed how my intentions affected the form of my body. When I experienced lots of energy, I moved my body in all manner of directions as happiness, passion, and vitality flowed through me. In the last thirty minutes of nonstop dancing, I experienced tiredness setting in. Then I moved slowly, at times allowing my head to hang down toward my knees. I glanced at my watch to see how much longer the session would last. I noticed discomfort and aches arising in my body. At the end of the session, I sat quietly for a few minutes so that rest and relaxation permeated my whole body. I left the dance hall feeling renewed, refreshed, and revitalized.

PRACTICE: DHARMA DANCING

Try to listen to a wide range of music, in particular different types of world music. If there is a music tradition that you already like, try to listen to a greater range of music within that tradition. It is important to give yourself the opportunity to listen fully to a piece of music as a meditation until you overcome any initial resistance. Habit often determines what we like or don't like, thus denying us the opportunity to listen wholeheartedly to unfamiliar or familiar music.

Put together a collection of music to fit the four kinds described here and to reflect the different moods. Try to listen and dance to the music for at least a half hour to give yourself an opportunity to go deep into the music and simultaneously deep into the dance. Remember to breathe mindfully while dancing, and stay steady despite any tiredness and discomfort, especially after a long session of continuous dance.

At the end of such a session, sit on a chair, or cross-legged on the floor, or lie on your back, and remain perfectly still for five minutes. Dharma Dancing treats music as a meditation for self-knowledge as well as physical, mental, and emotional health. Music acts as a remarkable resource for a clear and joyful connection with existence. It is truly food from the gods.

Dissolving

We often appreciate the opportunity to share with a friend or counselor some of our deeper experiences. Such communication helps us to understand more clearly what is going on within us. If we do not have such an opportunity to share our problems, then we often find ourselves thinking about our feelings in an attempt to make sense of what is going on. Thinking about our painful feelings often keeps us at a distance from them. Our feelings can contract around a particular issue that is unresolved. We keep thinking about the matter, which only strengthens our contraction around it. The painful feelings will have a location in the body, often in the chest, stomach, or diaphragm area. When we contract around an issue we can't think about much else. The unpleasant emotion acts like a fuel for our thoughts.

We easily forget the close and intimate relationship between our emotional life and our physical life. If we wish to dissolve an unwelcome contraction, we will probably need to attend to its location in the body. There are a few invaluable points here to bear in mind to make this clear within. For example, we feel disturbed or troubled about something. Can we turn our attention to the location in the body where we experience the feelings or emotions that disturb us? It is rather obvious what the matter is but thinking about it rarely gets to the root of it.

In a celebrated talk by the Buddha, he addressed the Four Foundations of Mindfulness that he referred to as mindfulness of body, feeling, states of mind, and sense objects. In his discourse, the Buddha encouraged his students to see the "feelings in the feeling." This means turning the attention toward, and focusing directly into, the feeling. Comprehending what we feel contributes to a shift in pressure or tightness so that it unpacks and dissolves. The Buddha said that when we have explored our feelings and emotional life, we shall know what it means to "abide freely and independently in the world."

PRACTICE: FOCUSING ON FEELING

The following practical exercise will help dissolve contractions around painful feelings and thoughts.

Sit comfortably in a chair with a straight back and in a relaxed posture. Close your eyes and turn your attention inward to see if there is a particular place or location in your body where you experience an unpleasant feeling. It could be in your chest, stomach, or another part of your body. Notice the outer edges of that feeling, the center of it. Stay quietly focused and in touch with its location in your body.

What is that feeling telling you? How would you describe it? Experience the feeling in your body. Describe that feeling in one or two words. In the direct experience of the contact with the feeling and the bare description, is there something you need to be clear about?

What do you need to understand here? What insight is needed to resolve the issue? Various thoughts and conclusions may arise in answer to these questions. A genuine insight or moment of clarity will make some kind of qualitative shift in the feeling, temporary or long-standing. This is an invaluable practice.

Let any understanding that emerges rest within. Avoid indulging in unpleasant feelings or emotions. Bear in mind what you see clearly. The understanding may show itself simply and directly: Acceptance. Change. Letting Go. Making Contact With. Avoiding. Starting. Finishing. Patience. Taking One Day at a Time. Endurance. Remembering to Breathe Mindfully. Dance. If you feel unsure or confused, turn your attention back to the bare feeling, noticing again which part of your body experiences the feeling. Explore that region of your body again with a bare description.

We can become overwhelmed when we contemplate the different things we feel are wrong with our life. The desire for things to be different can produce stress or despair as pressure mounts. At such times, we need to talk with someone who offers wise counsel, and to focus on the feeling to see it as just a temporary one, no matter how intense.

I have noticed that a person's capacity to stay steady with what they are feeling can become a catalyst for inner change. "What are you feeling right now?" is a profound question, but we forget that it is the ability to center very directly on the feeling in the body that matters, rather than lots of description about how we are feeling. It isn't easy to keep the attention on the feeling. We may deliberately focus on an area in the body, only to rebel or react against it, possibly releasing a storm of emotional agitation. If that happens, then engaging in creative free movement, perhaps to music, will help to channel the energy until we sense we have the capacity to focus on the bare location in the body of the contracted feeling or emotion. By developing the practice of penetrating into dissolution of such feelings, we can rediscover a sense of wholeness.

When everything goes well with our life, we can sometimes hardly believe the way things have come together. Then we start imagining that everything will start going wrong for us. Feelings of doubt or fear emerge, telling us that it could all go painfully wrong, that nothing will work out, and that we will soon be back where we started. Once again, we have to focus on this feeling, and dissolve it, or engage in creative expression that will shift the energy that is latching onto these negative feelings and thoughts. We need the strength of humility to accept that things do often simply "fall into place" in life. We need to focus right on that feeling of tiresome doubt until we stop believing in it, even if the doubt arises again out of habit. We may need to reapply our attention to what we feel in the body a number of times before we develop this practice fully.

This dissolution of difficult issues contributes to health and a sense of wholeness. This sense of wholeness means there is no separation whatsoever between the rest of the world and ourselves. It is the realization that everything belongs together. When we feel fragmented, we become disconnected from the world. We view the world as a place from which we can get what we want for ourselves, through maximizing pleasure and minimizing pain. We often remain unaware of the sense of wholeness and fullness that we participate in moment to moment. We have the capacity to experience this through an expansive and enlivened awareness of existence.

When we don't feel connected with the fullness of life, there is a fragmentation that we believe in as a truth. We have contracted around something that seems to cut us off from the fullness of things. We obsess about ourselves, another person, or an issue to the degree that nothing else matters. Mindfulness practice contributes to the embracing of all experiences so that we understand they belong to the totality of life. There is a self-deception that takes place when we think we can know personal fulfillment on a daily basis while remaining stuck in conflict and anguish. We realize fulfillment through embracing the challenges of life instead of contracting around problems.

We have become used to dividing the day up into fragments of time, rather than appreciating that there are no divisions in the day, no divisions in life, and that we impose time upon life until we become bewitched by dates and by the belief in the continuity of time. There is no inherent truth in a time-bound existence. We forget this and, in this forgetfulness, we experience a complex and hurried life with different events competing for our attention. Skillful, creative movement and the skillful dissolving of difficult issues reveal a wise response to daily tasks and enable us to meditate on wholeness, on the fullness of things that is immediately available. In such realization, everything else falls into place.

EXERCISE: DANCING IN SILENCE

Dance slowly and mindfully to pay respect to Silence. Move every single part of the body. Feel every stretch, every limb, and every sensation in the body. Feel the breathing as you move. Be in no hurry. Stretch out every single sinew possible so that mindfulness, exercise, and dance all meet together in prayer-like movement. Then play music while allowing the body to convey the message of the music.

EXERCISE: REFLECTING ON DISSOLUTION

Sit quietly in a comfortable posture and take time to reflect on the countless daily experiences of dissolving. The flame of a match. The end of the day. From feeling energetic to being tired. Sugar in a cup of tea. Food dissolving in the stomach. Dissolution of a cloud in the sky. Develop a practice of acknowledgment of what comes goes and goes, no matter how trivial. What forms will dissolve, what arises will pass. Make it a regular practice so that you get used to such changes.

practicing renunciation

Renunciation of Desire

There are times in our lives when we find it difficult to accept hurt and disappointment, and this brings about a kind of energetic reaction that has its consequences. For example, John had spent more than five years in a close personal relationship with a single mother. Being a warm-hearted person, he gave considerably of himself, as well as of his financial resources, to the mother and her young daughter. The family unit shared much in common.

One day, rather forcefully and in a detached way, the mother decided to bring an end to the relationship, leaving John feeling shocked and devastated. He returned to his apartment in the city, hoping she would have a change of heart. Unable to cope, he went out to a nightclub and met a woman with whom he became sexually involved, but whom he didn't love or particularly care for. Within a few weeks he reported that he felt even more unhappy; he felt a dropping away of his energy and a disappointment in himself for becoming involved with another woman. "I've lost my direction. I wake up wondering what I am doing lying beside this woman," he told me.

He had believed that he could have a short-term affair to get over his partner, but instead it left him feeling unhappy and wondering how he could extricate himself from this affair. He felt shell-shocked and exhausted. He thought that his new lover would help make him feel better, but he felt worse. He didn't need to transfer his attention to another woman. It didn't occur to him that the single mother had the right to end her relationship with him at any time—with or without reason. Nor did it occur to him that he had to give up all desire and clinging to the past to get on with his life.

Renunciation of Materialism

Renunciation of desire and clinging has an equally important function to play in the material world. In the 1980s, the term "upwardly mobile" became widely used in Western society, as the political and corporate world encouraged us to increase significantly our standard of living. We adopted the belief that increasing our standard of living provides proof that we are doing well in the world. We now seriously need to revise this way of thinking. This requires an honest examination of our priorities, so that we replace materialistic desires with our relationship to a larger sense of purpose and vision.

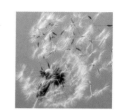

Instead of thinking in terms of being "upwardly mobile," we should consider becoming "downwardly mobile," and adopt a philosophy of life that values less rather than more, contentment rather than desire, a connection with what is, rather than chasing after what we want. When we ground ourselves in the here and now, it takes the pressure off our desire for accomplishments. This will take some of the pressure off our existence and, equally, off the disappearing resources of the natural world. Such a change in thought would be a revolutionary step, challenging our educationalists, economists, the business community, and politicians.

Inspiration

Where are we to turn to for inspiration and guidance in finding a different way of being in the world with different priorities? When we cut through the rites and rituals of religion, we can discover authentic religious insights that genuinely emphasize renunciation as an indispensable feature of the spiritual life. Jesus stated it simply: "First seek the Kingdom of God and all else will be added on to you."

If we are to take mindfulness and the spiritual life seriously, then we have to address acts of renunciation, no matter how uncomfortable. Any cursory examination of the old religious texts reveals breathtaking stories of self-sacrifice and renunciation of worldly security for a sense and experience of something greater. We need to take notice of the lives of monks and nuns, who have taken vows of poverty. Their acts of

renunciation have inspired generations of men and women to give up the material world. We may understandably wonder what we can do to express renunciation while at the same time keeping a roof over our heads and paying the various bills. It often seems that the world of the religious renunciant and the householder are far apart.

If we are to be serious about our spiritual practice, then we need to examine our relationship to consumer culture. For example, a ruthless spring cleaning at home can mark the sign of an initiative to live with less. If we set ourselves to this task, no doubt we will experience regret about things that we have thrown out or given away. That's part of the challenge of renunciation. In other words, it hurts. Mother Teresa, the great missionary of Calcutta, once told me in one of our meetings: "Give, give, give. True giving begins when it hurts to give."

If we are willing to push at our edges, to challenge our consciousness, we have the opportunity to open to a bigger dimension of things. We have to go against the current, and not be swept along by the mainstream of a self-centered, materialistic culture. We need to learn to question what matters and to forge a new direction with consciousness. It is a bold thing to do, but without it spirituality is meaningless.

Everyday Living

There are two forms of renunciation and both matter equally. The first is the act of giving up the thing itself. Perhaps we are working extraordinarily hard to pay an exorbitant rent on a very comfortable apartment. Is it worth working oneself to death to pay for it? Are we ready to be downwardly mobile? Do we have the nerve to get something more affordable that is less beautiful to the eye? This would mean renunciation of certain comforts. Are we ready for that? I met a woman who had left her marriage and her detached home, given up her expensive holidays, her new car and yacht, to live in a one-room apartment, do secretarial work, and follow her heart. She reported that she had never felt happier in her life. After several years, she had never regretted the change, nor missed what she had renounced. Many people, in both cities and rural areas, live modestly and genuinely experience contentment with little.

They make few demands on themselves to make a lot of money, or demands on others to provide them with financial resources.

The second kind of renunciation is that of giving up the desire to control or grasp onto things. If we learn to feel a certain lightness toward all that we own and enjoy, we can take a deep interest in the nonmaterial realm. This means forging a different kind of relationship to life, one in which we appreciate the forms that come to the eye rather than the desire to pursue and own.

EXERCISE: PRACTICING RENUNCIATION

Make a list of what you can give up as an expression of your determination to live a free and conscious life.

Start with what is relatively easy: this might include letting go of the desire to get a new car or to own one, selling works of art to give money to charity, giving up surplus books, cosmetics, cigarettes, alcohol, junk food, and luxury goods—anything from the vast array of superfluous items that fill the home.

Do you dare go further than this? What else can you renounce to find the bare truth of existence? Your relationship? Your children? Your wealth? Your precious possessions? Your career? Your known existence? All of these? None of them? Nothing should be excluded from the list. Everything has to be put onto that list, no matter how impossible it may seem to contemplate.

Consider what would be easier to let go of and what would be the most difficult to live without.

EXERCISE: RENOUNCING UNHEALTHY SPEECH

Practice renouncing a particular pattern of speech, such as the need to complain, express anger, repeat gossip, or indulge in memories. Start each day with a commitment to let go of the impulse to use unwise speech. Try to make your speech unhurried, calm, and thoughtful, even in the face of provocation, so that in the renunciation of unhealthy speech, wholesome speech comes naturally.

examining objects

Our world is full of objects. Think of the number of different objects that come to your senses every day. You couldn't possibly count them. Remember how many different things you see on a daily basis or how many things you hear. Then add to that all the different smells, tastes, and things you touch. We might also describe all that goes on in our mind as objects as well, because thoughts, attitudes, states of mind, memories, plans, and the whole range of feelings, emotions, and reactions exist as objects of our attention.

Objects may therefore be physical or mental, sentient or insentient. Day in and day out, we have become involved with objects to the point that we might describe our life as going from one object to another, moment after moment. There are times when the importance of an object is brought sharply into focus. The following scenario will be familiar to many of us. You overslept and are running late. You have

a quick shower, a cup of coffee, and gather together the necessary papers for a meeting. Hurrying to get out of the house, you realize you don't have the key to the car in your pocket. You panic. For that moment, that tiny object, a small piece of metal, matters more than anything else. Racing back upstairs, you rummage around in yesterday's clothes, search the kitchen table, the laundry basket, and the desk with the computer. No car key. Agitation, anxiety, and wild thoughts take over. You finally spot the key next to the telephone—you had received a call just as you got home from work last night and put the key down next to the telephone. Your whole body relaxes. Inner peace returns and you return to the car. Forgetfulness can trigger panic that could have been avoided through mindfulness.

Our relationship to "things" affects our sense of well-being. We might give an object—whether it is a person, item, or idea—great significance; alternatively, we might dismiss it altogether, or adopt a position somewhere between the two. Sometimes we claim that an object causes our happiness or is responsible for our unhappiness. We forget the layers of projection, desire, and attachment associated with objects that originate in us. We grant significance to objects and give them power to make an impact on us. Our mind swings from elation to despair, according to the way we see things. Mindfulness practice is learning to see objects as objects, free from desires and needs, and to explore the interconnectedness of all things and experiences. This liberates us from the pull of objects during the day. At night we naturally strive to be free of this through sleep.

Sleep is the cessation of influence of everything upon us. When we lie in our bed at night we don't want to be thinking about all the things we should have done and didn't do during the day. We don't want to be remembering childhood experiences or conversations in the office, nor do we want to be planning what we have to do tomorrow or where we hope to be a year from now. We have no interest in seeing more things, or hearing more sounds. Sleep means the temporary end of the world, of the known, and of all objects in the field of consciousness.

Getting to Sleep

There is a large number of people who find it distressingly difficult to get to sleep easily. The following four considerations may help you to make a relaxed transition from the world of objects to deep sleep.

1 Limit your intake of stimulants such as caffeine, tobacco, and sugar, especially shortly before going to bed.

2 Avoid eating a heavy meal for at least two hours before bedtime. Instead, choose easily digestible, nutritious foods. Some foods, for example bananas and lettuce, are particularly recommended as having sleep-inducing properties.

3 In bed, posture is important. Relax your whole body into the mattress. Lie there mindfully, quietly maximizing the sense of rest. Consider also the direction you sleep in and the kind of mattress you use. Experiment. See what works so that you can enter the channel from the waking state through the dream world into deep sleep.

4 The greatest contribution to a good night's sleep is a relaxed attitude toward events during the day—a mindful attitude during the day can contribute greatly.

We can work ourselves so hard that it causes an imbalance in our lives; we experience a massive dissipation of our energy that leaves us feeling helpless and frustrated. We have no energy for the activities of the day, and too much conscious energy to sleep at night. We become locked in a merciless cycle.

A friend told me that he worked far too many hours from dawn until late at night as a principal in a school. He said, "I never found time to relax. I didn't know how to relax. I took home the problems of the staff and pupils. My life was my work with no time for anything else. Eventually I collapsed emotionally, mentally, and physically. Some mornings I stayed in bed, not having the strength to reach across to answer the bedside telephone. I had no willpower to get up. Things seemed worse when I tried." The principal, who had to take sabbatical leave, began to practice meditation. He would sit in a Buddha-like

position in bed, on top of his pillows, initially using the headboard as a backrest. Instead of trying to move, he practiced to be a Buddha by staying motionless and upright. As time went by, he found within himself a natural conservation of energy through stillness. He reported that through keeping his hands very still, whether sitting upright or lying down in bed, he began to feel the slow recovery of his energy. "Stillness gave me my life back," he said.

The practical benefits of mindfulness include taking care to conserve energy, and not dissipating it through restless movement, no matter how well we are. We practice, really practice, to remember to be less forgetful or less speedy. The principal believed he was indispensable to the school, though he would never admit this to himself or his colleagues. He worked and worked until his body gave up in protest. Genuine mindfulness will help to reveal to us such unhealthy patterns and give us the power to make changes.

Time and Space as Objects

Humans have been in existence for perhaps only ten thousand years, while scientists continue to debate the age of the earth in terms of billions of years. Our visit to this world may last a hundred years or fewer. Such reflections on time help us to put things into perspective. It is also worth remembering that we are each only a single person out of a species of more than six billion.

Rather than taking a long-term and expansive view of things, we tend to indulge in what is trivial and insignificant. We need a genuine re-evaluation of the way we use our senses, not just employing them for self-gratification. Instead of going from seeing to having, we should explore the practice of "in the seeing there is just the seeing, in the hearing there is just the hearing," as the Buddha taught. Take this moment. Keep the body still. Let the eyes explore all the different colors, shapes, and forms visible to you in this moment. It is a realm of interrelated forms that no artist can capture. In the seeing there is just the seeing. Each of the senses reveals a remarkable realm different from the other senses, yet are all interconnected.

We have five sensory organs: eyes, ears, nose, tongue, and skin. Each is quite remarkable in its own right. If we sit still with our eyes closed, and then slowly but gently lift our eyelids up, we will find that simply being aware of what is immediately in front of us is truly a remarkable event in itself. We tend to take this "sense door" for granted, rather than finding immense appreciation within ourselves for our capacity to see.

When we hear sounds passing through the air, their vibrations travel through our ears and our body. Consciousness registers the sounds, recognizes them, and sometimes defines and labels them. It doesn't matter what we listen to, or what object comes to our sense doors; but it is important to appreciate how extraordinary such an event is. Ownership of a few objects, in the light of this event, is of little consideration.

Mindfulness and Objects

First, we need to bring mindfulness to bear on objects so that we have a balanced and wise understanding of them. Second, we can explore mindfulness of the subject (ourself, our awareness) that makes contact with the object. This mindfulness will help us to stop investing too much of ourselves and projecting our desires onto objects.

That means we practice being here and now without seizing upon any objects. We gain a sense of the full expanse of things without making one thing more important than something else. We are not pushed or pulled by our desires; our body and mind are at rest, free from the forces of attraction and aversion. To help achieve mindfulness, it is important to consider the following questions:

• What is so important about objects that we have granted some of them such overwhelming importance in our life?
• Why have we made such a fetish of objects?
• Why do we feel compelled to buy new things and replace old ones?
• Why are we so infatuated with our thoughts? Why have they become such an object of interest, determining our view of events? We lose sight of the original

nature of the subject through getting immersed in things and thoughts that distort our capacity to realize the original nature of consciousness, bright, clear, and unsoiled.

It is extraordinary that the subject stands indispensable at the center of daily life, yet we put all our values onto objects, changing and ephemeral, that can only become substantial to us through the significance we impart to them. Subject and object belong to each other, support each other, and depend upon each other. The deathless light of realization effortlessly embraces subject and object.

EXERCISE: SETTLING THE MIND

Treat going to sleep as a meditation in relaxation. Experience the full length of your body in the horizontal posture.

Allow every part of your body to relax into the mattress. Stay completely still so that your mind is settled quietly into your body.

EXERCISE: DEALING WITH DESIRE

When you next feel desire for an object, be mindful of any feelings you are projecting onto the object and any personal investment you are making.

How dependent are you on obtaining this car, television, or other item?

Ask yourself why possession of the object really matters. As the desire takes hold, remember to breathe mindfully. This will help to clear your mind and the object should lose the significance you are projecting onto it.

2: mindfulness of energy

monitoring our energy

A mindful attitude to the energy in our body, mind, and heart involves its wise application in these three areas of our life. The depletion of energy in one area of our life can affect other areas, sometimes in dramatic ways. Many people report, for example, that when their heart goes out of their relationship or out of their work, they experience a significant lowering of energy and a fading of enthusiasm for any activity. For some, this is accompanied by a low sense of self-worth, a heaviness of heart, a dullness of mind, and a general lack of vitality in the body. The practice of mindfulness of energy aims to apply energy wisely and to avoid wasting energy or being subject to negative energy. This practice embraces five main areas.

1 Mindfulness of the Energy of Harmony

This energy gives a sense of inner peace throughout our whole being. We feel at ease, comfortable, and stable within our immediate environment. There is spaciousness in our outlook and a fullness to our life, whether active or not. In this inner = outer harmony, we place demands neither on the world nor on ourselves. We experience a natural equilibrium and balanced relationship with all of our senses. A well-adjusted person living with mindfulness and wisdom abides in this state as a daily norm, noticing that if it becomes disturbed this is only temporary. In deep spirituality, the liberation of the human being from inner problems reveals effortlessly this expansive sense of harmony with the field of existence.

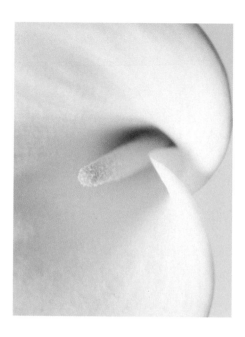

2 Mindfulness of the Energy of Attraction

Under the compelling influence of the force of attraction, we sometimes find ourselves pulled toward an idea, material object, or person, without the capacity to exercise restraint. Such compulsion can deplete our energy and be a bar to wise, mindful living. We sometimes fail to realize what we get ourselves into, and the painful consequences of going along with such a force. There is a simple trigger for this— namely, a pleasant feeling backed up with a tendency of mind, past behavior, and the force of desire, a combination that acts like a magnet.

The Buddha said that our activities can begin with a pleasant feeling and end up pleasant, begin with a pleasant feeling and end up painful, begin with a painful feeling and end up pleasant, or begin with a painful feeling and end up painful. Wisdom acts as a stabilizing element, allowing us to express our warm, loving feelings without them becoming an indulgence, a foolish habit, a tendency, or a sudden compulsion that brings about more distress at a later date. We develop this wisdom through learning deeply from past circumstances, developing the capacity to say "no" to an unhelpful attraction, and knowing our areas of vulnerability.

3 Mindfulness of the Energy of Aversion

To find out more about ourselves, we could write out a list of what we don't like. It might be a short or long list. Many of us have a tendency to find fault around us or within, believing that the cause for our aversion lies totally with the object. In the midst of this negative energy of aversion, it seems to be the self-evident truth that goes unquestioned in our mind. If we bring mindfulness to bear on our perceptions, it will reveal to us that latent, unresolved aversion, born from the past, has simply latched onto an impression, such as something we see or hear. Our aversion may have nothing to do with what is happening around us. The way we react tells us more about ourselves than the object or person against whom we are reacting.

If we are always complaining, we may find that friends and loved ones do not wish to be in our company. There is a natural resistance to spending time in the company of those who constantly find fault, complain, or seem cynical. Negative energy colors and distorts our way of looking at things, sometimes intensifying to the point of anger, tantrums, and rage as the aversion invades our speech and body. It can become debilitating, crippling what is meaningful, joyful, and beautiful. Stuck in such negative patterns, we harm ourselves far more than anyone else could ever do. Mindfulness practice is the commitment to stop giving authority to the energy of aversion. We need to be mindful of the underlying issues when we complain.

4 Mindfulness of the Energy to Initiate Action

In the first three kinds of energy, we observed how influential the inner life is on the levels of energy that we experience. There is also the energy for action, for healthy, wholesome, and ethical action that enables energy to flow easily and freely. We often imagine that our daily commitments are a pressure. If we learn to appreciate and enjoy the details of daily life, we can relax around our responsibilities. With a full, rich and diverse day, this energy enables us to sleep well at night.

It flows best when there is no resistance to the task, or dependency on the outcome. The action for change then carries its own validity and authenticity. No resistance and no dependency make all the difference. We should never forget this. Energy gradually becomes depleted when we engage in doing something with an underlying resistance to the task at hand. This resistance incapacitates us. Experiencing that free flow of connection allows for energetic renewal. The Buddhist tradition emphasizes the value of training the mind to be really here and now, not clinging to memory or to expectations about the future. Through mindfulness of the here and now, we conserve energy in heart, mind, and body that otherwise would get wasted by slipping excessively into memories and plans.

When we make changes, we enter into the field of intention, action, and result. The state of our inner life and our relationship to intention, action, and result are inextricably bound up together, and it is this understanding that makes such a huge difference in our life. For example, if we know ourselves well and the world around us equally well, we see that the results of our actions are not in our hands, but are linked to various conditions, both within and without. If we don't know ourselves well, we may place high expectations upon ourselves so that we end up feeling disappointed with the outcome of our actions. Alternatively, we may have a low sense of our capacity to initiate changes, thus barely failing to get an intention off the ground.

Intention, action, and result require a focused energy. Meditation helps to ground us in the present and to conserve inner energy so that pleasurable and painful memories weaken, if not exhaust themselves. Our wasted energy then quietly fades from consciousness.

5 Mindfulness of Our Energy Through Contact

We sometimes marvel at the sudden and unexpected release of energy that we can experience throughout our whole being. We hardly realize the amount of energy or vitality that is contained in our cells. A single simple experience can spark such a release, such as a chance meeting with an old friend.

It can take only a single momentary contact through the eyes for a sudden change to take place within that can brighten up our sense of our whole being— enough to shake off tiredness, boredom, and irritability. A boost to our emotional life can boost our energy generally. Equally, a painful emotional experience can have a negative impact on us physically.

Wise living involves learning to apply energy as fully as possible without resistance, and learning to conserve energy through meditation, focused attention, cultivation of calmness, and appropriate time for rest and sleep. We need to know the kind of contact that sparks and develops energy and the kind of contact that drains energy. We can then examine what we need to cultivate and what we need to overcome in our lives. If we keep feeling tired, it often indicates that we are digging unnecessarily into our resources through lack of nourishment and renewal of our heart, mind, and body. Frequent tiredness is a warning signal, and one or two minor changes can usually make all the difference.

13: developing a daily practice

There is never any guarantee that we can keep to a stable, day-to-day routine. Some days, we may be called upon to extend ourselves farther than we would normally go, for example, to give comfort to a friend who is suffering. Yet, we don't have to push ourselves to extremes, or endeavor to stay within a comfort zone that gradually acts like a shell around our existence. There is a great wonder to life revealing itself.

Sometimes I am up late at night, because I am working through the countless forms of energy that manifest on a daily basis. To move our hand up to pick up the kettle to make a cup of tea is a remarkable expression of application of energy, no matter how many times a day we do it. Mindfulness practice keeps us in touch with the flow of the energy of life.

Wake up to a new joy today with
the new rays of the sun.
To a clean life which is good,
beautiful, and sparkling with love.

The wind of peace today
Carries the fragrance of the flowers
of eternity.

RABINDRANATH TAGORE

I want to watch on television. Sometimes I get up early because I have a plane to catch or I need a little more time to prepare for something special happening during the day.

I rarely go to bed after 2 A.M., however, or get up much before 5 A.M. It occurs to me that in all my life I have rarely been up and about at 3 or 4 o'clock in the morning. Those two or three hours—we call them the "small" hours—are virtually unknown to most of us.

You might like to try on some occasion to visit the small hours. Go for a walk around your neighborhood just as it is becoming light, before the traffic has started and people set off for work. There are people who are active at this time: the emergency services, those involved in cleaning and preparing buildings for the arrival of the regular staff, news and postal workers, but it remains a curious sort of time when the familiar appears unfamiliar and the ordinary strange.

You can think of your life as being like a day. You are born at dawn, you grow in the morning, and reach maturity at noon. The afternoon represents your adult life, the evening your retirement, and then night falls and you find peace. The small hours are then like the time in the womb, or from the other perspective, your eternal rest. For those who believe in reincarnation the small hours have a particular meaning as standing for the time in between death and rebirth. Not surprisingly, one group of people who often make particular use of this time are those who live the monastic life. Monks and nuns of different traditions rise during the night to spend time in reading and prayer while the rest of the world sleeps.

EXERCISE: BEING AWARE OF ATTRACTION

Be aware of the pleasant feeling that supports attraction and the pull toward something.

If inner wisdom says to drop the pull, then remember to breathe mindfully through the experience or remove yourself from the temptation.

Keep practicing this until the mind gains strength to overcome this force.

Remember that wisdom tells us when it is useful to move toward something and when it is preferable to avoid it. For example, we might move toward eating some fruit when we are hungry and avoid eating a bar of chocolate.

EXERCISE: BEING AWARE OF AVERSION

Be aware of the unpleasant feeling that supports aversion and the reaction against something.

Be aware of thoughts, memories, and old attitudes influencing the reaction.

Ask yourself honestly whether aversion is the appropriate response to resolving a situation.

See if you can distinguish between an unpleasant feeling and reactivity. For example, your flight is delayed for four hours, forcing you to miss a business meeting. You can experience agitated feelings and views or take the opportunity to relax into the present moment.

Spirit of God, make us open to
others in listening,
Generous to others in giving
And sensitive to others
in praying.

FROM THE CHRISTIAN TRADITION

OBSERVING OUR sexual energy

Looking Beyond Appearances

We all know that beauty is only skin deep, but the relationship between the self and the skin or physical form is very complex. We may envy the striking features of another, their sensuous presence and elegant manner, but that surface appearance may hide many difficulties that lie within. There are often unwelcome expectations and pressures upon people who are perceived to be beautiful. They are treated as gods or goddesses, rather than ordinary people living ordinary lives like the rest of us. They become icons of our imagination, and this often leaves them feeling isolated and perhaps lonely, and uncertain about their intelligence. We have to learn to see such people as people.

We live in a culture that has elevated sex into the realms of projection and imagination—sex has become detached from the simple realities of human warmth and love. We have intense expectations of sex and build up our own picture of the ideal woman or man. Countless magazines feature beautiful people on their covers, who are attractive, desirable, and sensual. These images make the general public—who don't go to expensive hairdressers, or wear designer clothes, or have exquisite photographs of themselves touched up—look ordinary. Many advertisements for all kinds of products—a car, a pair of running shoes, a type of coffee—communicate via sexual innuendo. Countless books, television programs, sports stars, and entertainers carry the allure of sex. Even television news broadcasters have to be beautiful, although this has nothing to do with the content of the news that they are reporting.

Inner strength and confidence evolve when we can see the emptiness of appearances and can stay in touch with knowing bare actuality rather than the layers of projection upon people or situations. It is the practice of seeing physical life as physical life, feelings as feelings, states of mind as states of mind, and a human being simply as that. Such a practice helps to keep us steady and clear so that we don't become overwhelmed with the unconscious force of attraction that distorts direct and clear communication. This practice requires concentrated attention, calm abiding, and equanimity, either when we are in contact with an attractive person, or with a person who clearly feels attracted to us. This inner calmness needs to express itself in the way we talk, sit, walk, and stand.

If we are to communicate effectively, we also must learn to listen. If we cannot listen to one another, then we should not expect somebody else to listen to us. This same principle applies equally in lovemaking with a caring, supportive, and sensitive partner. One of our greatest needs is to feel understood. Few experiences in life trigger so much agitation and emotional hardship as when we feel misunderstood. Sometimes we need to choose our words very carefully when discussing sensitive matters concerning our perceptions, feelings, and views, especially if they concern the person we are talking to. In delicate matters, such as feedback about intimacy and sex, we have to be wary of treading on the other person's toes. Our high level of expectations in sexual matters means that we often feel vulnerable to criticism. Instead of finding it helpful, we may withdraw into a shell of self-protection.

We often carry fixed ideas about intimate relationships where age, gender, physical appearance, size, class, and cultural and ethnic background are concerned. We project our preferences onto a couple, for example if there is a big age gap, and if we don't approve of a particular relationship, we tend to make some simplistic psychological analysis.

As a society, we have to learn to accept and understand people's choices in matters of the heart. It is important that two people in a relationship feel supported, not judged, by family and friends, no matter how difficult it might seem to understand why they are together.

Sexual Intimacy

Every year, new books appear in our bookstores on ways and means to cultivate a fulfilling sex life. A combination of love, genuine respect, adventure, and a variety of positions for lovemaking can certainly enhance the experience of sexual intimacy. However, it is not always easy or comfortable for two people to talk about such matters together and lovemaking can often become routine. One partner may feel content with the frequency and form of the lovemaking, but if the other feels frustrated, disappointed, or even used, then a fresh perspective on how to develop a comfortable and worthwhile intimacy can be vital.

Spirituality and sexual activity can come together as a sacred practice, not just as the initiation of different positions and energies. It is the loving and caring attitude of mind that matters above all else. A couple had read a number of books about exploring and developing sexual energy. They read about Tantra, the ancient Hindu and Buddhist practice of harnessing sexual energy for spiritual depths. At home, late one afternoon, the couple, who had developed a deep relationship over two years, spontaneously shared some experiences with each other that led them both into a long, gentle period of lovemaking. They reported how, in the midst of lovemaking, they simultaneously became extraordinarily aware of a sense of God around them, as if they were two loving energies utterly interfused while in the presence of God. "We made love while God watched over us," commented one partner later. Afterward, they described the experience as a very profound and beautiful moment. There is a depth to lovemaking that we can touch upon that transcends the ordinary and the everyday. It is through attention and devotion to each other that we begin to realize a fusion

The value of this kind of prayer is that it is "objective." People say they don't pray because they cannot think of what to pray about, when they usually mean they can think of so many issues that they do not know where to start. Make a list of the things that concern you and that you want to pray about and give them a time of their own during your week. Dedicate a particular day to a concern and use each prayer moment to recall it and pray on it. Do not worry if it all begins to sound rather mechanical and ... structure you are giving yourself ... to be flexible about it. You cannot improvise upon a musical instrument before you have learned how to play it!

Be careful, though, not to fill a busy day with busy prayers. Make sure that the time you take for prayer always includes a few moments of silence. You are the subject of God's prayer and he may want to communicate with you specifically in the midst of your busy life. Prayer is always a time for attention to what is going on around you, not indifference to it. There must be something wrong with praying for the rain forest because it is midday on a Wednesday, while some relationship in your workplace collapses or a colleague is in need.

Praying at set times is a valuable discipline, but we need also to understand that prayer is not just something we do now and then but rather a way of doing and being all the time. In other words, we need to be able to find the eternal in the ordinary.

Think again about your daily routine. It may involve some traveling that you could try to think of as a pilgrimage. Perhaps it involves some kind of routine that you could use meditatively to quietly recite a "list" prayer.

... of life, energy, and mystery in such unity. Two lovers can then rest together in great silence and great space.

It is one of the extensive problems of conventional religion that there has been a separation of flesh from mind and soul. In true intimacy, these conceptual divisions melt away, leaving only immeasurable love. In such love, there is no one to give love and no one to receive it. Both partners find themselves in an inseparable, indivisible love where the self of one and the self of the other blend like milk and wa...

Born out of a caring respect and flowing energy, the act of lovemaking can be a transcendental experience. Such experiences act as a catalyst for deep in... into an utterly integrated existence, a profound sense of universal unity and h...ony. These precious moments, freed from the egotism and inhibitions that are ... up with sex, enter into the realms of mystical discovery, a spiritual realiza... act of intimate love belongs to a deeper dimension than we realize.

The interconnection of two lovers, who are passionately and sensitively s... of each other, reveals something of the way things are in the great field ... namely that all is interconnected and intimate. Yet we need to be mindfu... not "grab hold of" deep experiences—whether we call them divine, tra... or tantric—with the aim of repeating them, as this places expectations on ... or our partner. The sweetness of the memory then becomes a hindrance a... for repetition.

Our mindfulness practices remind us to develop a calm and clear relation... present as well as with the past. Sometimes we have a significant experie... with another, and we move on far too quickly. We need to make time for...

Silence belongs to the
substance of sanctity.
In silence and hope are
formed the strength of
the saints.

THOMAS MERTON

reflection on the great value of the experience. We do not need to try to resurrect the experience, but should instead acknowledge the depth of it and the greater understanding that it reveals about ourselves and life itself.

Lovemaking can become a sacred act, a religious experience, a revelation of the wonder of life, when two people cultivate kindness and friendship over the course of time and melt into unitive love. This requires a willingness to reflect wisely and sensitively on relationships, so that we can draw the wisdom out of our important experiences. Our relationship to sexuality deserves reflection.

- *Are we content with the way things are?*
- *What is our attitude toward sexual relationships?*
- *Are there areas that we need to be more conscious about?*
- *What shows wisdom in sexuality?*
- *What are some of the conditions that contribute to it?*

Such questions are beneficial in helping us to find out who we are. Drawing upon our experience of sexual intimacy, we can convert it to develop a deep understanding about this important feature of life. If we neglect to examine our relationship to sexuality, it may lead to pain, anguish, or problems in how we express our sexual energy. Relationships and sexual intimacy lack the power to inhibit freedom and awakening. It is instead, the other way around—sexual experience can contribute to our liberation as much as solitude and vows of celibacy can. If we are relaxed and comfortable without sexual energy, we can experience much joy, peace of mind, and an expansive sense of unity with life.

EXERCISE: SHARING INTIMACY

Remember that sexual intimacy is a way to express love, not an ego trip around your performance.

In intimacy, check that you are listening and caring for the other person as much as for yourself.

Be willing to share your feelings and appreciation with your partner.

Treat each moment as a fulfillment rather than being goal-orientated.

EXERCISE: BEING RESPECTFUL

Be watchful of feeding sexual fantasies and projecting them onto an individual. Try to see and pay respect to the whole person.

Pay attention to unconscious energies that express themselves as flirting, or affectionate touch that may be unwelcome to and unwanted by another, or simply inappropriate.

Keep communication warm and clear so the other person feels safe.

attending to health

Health

Our health matters a great deal to us. Our lifestyle has an enormous influence on our health, though we sometimes deny this by adopting the view that hereditary factors and genetic influence determine our well-being. It is important to consider

such past influence upon our lives, but mindfulness practices encourage us to participate in the healing process rather than treat ourselves as victims of circumstance. Since many of us will find ourselves in a hospital at some point in our lives, it is important to realize that we do not have to take up a passive role in such a situation.

Western medicine tends to concentrate exclusively on the physical aspects of the person rather than attending to the whole person. The patient finds him- or herself submitting to treatments such as surgery, chemotherapy, or radiation as the primary forms of treatment. There is little or no guidance for the patient to help to heal him- or herself. The Western model tends to be in sharp contrast to other older traditions of

medicine in the East, which adopt a holistic approach and seek to treat the whole person. Patients can contribute to their own health and well-being through a variety of exercises, movements, breathing practices, meditation, visualizations, posture, music, and uplifting of the spirit.

For some patients it can be depressing lying in a bed 24 hours a day, waiting for treatment, or recovering from it, without any practices to develop to contribute to the healing process. We applaud the sophisticated equipment used for transforming life-threatening situations for patients, but we wish to empower ourselves at the time as well. Machines can't do that. Perhaps we have given too much authority to medical science and we need to take some of that back.

For example, we often attribute the general improvement in public health to the advances of medical science in the past century, instead of to the dramatic improvements that have resulted in a balanced diet, clean water, high standards of personal hygiene, healthier working conditions, and greatly improved sanitation. These kinds of social development have put an end to many infectious diseases that plagued Western nations for centuries.

Yet, we now face a new range of diseases that have grown with our current civilization—namely a wide range of cancers, heart disease, and obesity in the West. The underfed generations of the past have turned into the overfed generations of the present. The practice of mindfulness has a vital role to play in working to overcome the diseases that plague contemporary life. Prevention is always better than cure. Mindfulness works to develop factors that contribute to health and equally works to overcome conditions that contribute to ill health.

EXERCISE: MAKING A LITANY OR "LIST" PRAYER

• *Think of the objects that you make use of (or even make) every day at work or school or in your own home.*

• *Make an association between each one and some intention for prayer. You could do this on the basis of what the item looks like or is used for. For example, a pen could stand for communication between friends, relatives, or parties in dispute; a safe or locked cupboard could represent the inner mystery at the heart of all things; a corridor could represent the route to illumination. The more way-out the association is, the easier it will be to remember!*

• *Alternatively you could make a list finding a subject for prayer for each letter of the alphabet in turn: awareness, blessing, communication, devotion, and so on. The list is your list so you can do what you want with it, mixing concepts with names and so on. As you carry out some routine task, run through the list in your head, pausing briefly on each item to turn the remembering memory into a prayer.*

With the support of concentrated attention, mindfulness develops the power of the mind and awareness of body sensations to establish the resources that support great health. Overeating, and the consumption of junk food and alcohol, tire the body, making the heart work harder, swelling the arteries, and making us vulnerable to painful conditions that often affect one or more organs of the body. We see the impact on obese children, who often have to pay an emotional cost as well, at school and with their friends, for being overweight. (Health officials define obesity as 20 percent or more above average body weight for one's height.)

It is easy to dismiss people who are overweight as being greedy, while failing to look at the emotional factors affecting them, such as insecurity, boredom, lack of self-worth, feeling empty inside and uncared for from the outside. Alternatively, they may be responding to their failing to realize that they have a slow metabolism, or are simply heavy; generous in size, with great spirit and a big heart. It would be a much poorer place without them. We must take care to educate them about the causes and conditions that lead to obesity, and offer support to health and longevity.

Working with Pain

In his book *Full Catastrophe Living*, Jon Kabat-Zinn writes about the various ways and techniques that he used, teaching groups to enable hospital patients in the U.S. to face their pain, and reduce it. He set out a whole series of gentle exercises, suitable yoga postures, and forms of mindfulness that were able to contribute to their healing. Kabat-Zinn drew on the practice of Vipassana (insight) meditation and mindfulness developed in the Buddhist tradition that works directly with the experience of mind and body. With the encouragement of Buddhist meditation teachers who taught classes on mindfulness, people were able to significantly increase their capacity to deal with pain, improve their health, and reduce their emotional attitudes.

Patients trained their minds to deal with levels of pain—either pre-surgery or post-surgery—and the side effects of medication, or ongoing pain such as arthritis, and so on. Working with their pain, patients could overcome the despair that often became associated with their condition. Some of the exercises included in this book are those used by Dr. Kabat-Zinn.

Such health programs show the important role that the mind has to play in matters of health, not only in terms of living wisely to maximize health, but also as a significant contribution toward speedy healing of the body. Western medicine lags behind the medical traditions of other parts of the world that support the holistic view that the division of mind from body is artificial. Regular insight meditation points to a focused attention to work with and accommodate pain and changes in the physical condition. It is a matter of practice.

The Buddha said we practice to see body as body, or to see body in the body. In other words, the outer body consists of what we outwardly perceive—our gender, our height, our color, our age, our shape, our weight, and so on. To see the body in the body, we need to experience the bare sensations of body. Then we remain in touch with the bare elemental facts.

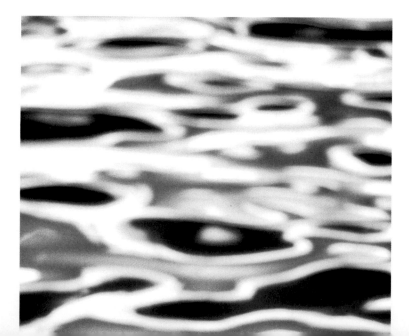

PRACTICE: HARMONIZING MIND AND BODY

The following insight meditation practice points to a direct relationship between mind and body. It is a practice that can be done daily, and is particularly beneficial for those who need to develop a harmonious relationship rather than an adversarial one between body and mind.

Place your attention directly on your body, starting with your head and going down to your feet. Attune your mindfulness to the immediate experience of the body sensations themselves. This is a subtle moment-to-moment practice, in which every single part of the body is experienced.

- Start at the top of your head, and move down your neck, shoulders, and arms.
- Then move down your back to your buttocks, and down your front to your genitals.
- Finally move from the top of each leg down to your toes.
- This scanning of your body may take anywhere from five to thirty minutes. Then reverse the process, starting from your feet and working up to the top of your head.
- During both the downward movement and the upward movement of the attention, experience all the sensations—vibrations, aches, pain, tingling, throbbing, itching, warm, coolness, numbness—the whole range of pleasant and unpleasant feelings. Be equaniminous toward the entire range of experiences of various body sensations.
- On completion of this practice, leave your body completely still. Be fully present to the presence of your whole body.
- Engaging in such a practice on a regular basis opens up cellular life, contributes to energy flowing more freely, and trains the mind to stay steady with pain, thus allowing for a practical application of the power of mindfulness to deal with the condition of body.
- Patients in hospitals can engage in the same practice lying down on their back or on their side. Various insight meditation centers offer guided meditations on tape for body/mind awareness.

Further Reading

The Mystic Vision: Daily Encounters with the Divine
Andrew Harvey. Published by Godsfield Press (1996)

The Oxford Book of Prayer
George Appleton (Ed.) Published by Oxford Paperbacks (2002)

Learn to Pray: a practical guide to enriching your life through prayer
Marcus Braybrooke. Published by Duncan Baird Publishers (2001)

Picture Acknowledgments

CORBIS: pp: 6, 8, 12, 16/17, 20, 23, 25, 30, 32, 35, 38, 39, 60, 64, 66, 68, 95, 98, 99, 100, 102, 110, 113b, 119, 120/121, 123, 125. IMAGE BANK: pp: 4, 5, 19, 28, 45, 46, 56, 61, 74, 79, 93, 108. GETTYONESTONE: pp: 2, 9, 18, 31, 34, 40, 50, 51, 54/55, 87, 88, 94, 112, 116, 117. NASA: p. 24. TELEGRAPH COLOUR LIBRARY: pp: 14, 15, 40, 47, 57, 65, 76, 86, 111.
COVER: CORBIS/STOCKMARKET.

EXERCISE: PERCEIVING PAIN

Some people experience particular pain in certain locations in the body. It can be a useful exercise to make a simple drawing of the body in the standing posture, then highlight the areas of pain and use colored pencils to draw the intensity of the pain. When scanning the body as part of your meditation practice, it is useful to spend more time in that area of pain, slowly moving the attention moment to moment to that location, so that mindfulness penetrates deeper and deeper into the pain before moving into the next area. Once a week, after several sessions of body scanning, you can then make further drawings to compare past and present experiences of the pain.

At times on retreats, people come to me to describe the kinds of pain they experience in their meditation posture, or daily physical pains they experience resulting from conditions to do with their health, age, posture, or personal history. I sometimes ask the retreatant: "Is your life outside the painful area?" Consciousness can become restricted to a painful locality to the degree that nothing else of significance goes on outside of it. Pain rests in a large area of non-pain. No-pain exposes pain. There is a life of nonpain outside of pain. It is not always easy to recognize and admit to pain. If we can admit to a little space around our pain, there is the opportunity to see the place of pain, notice its edges and challenge its intensity. Our meditation practice once again points to this holistic perception of pain.

INDEX

Movement

We have become used to moving our bodies in much the same way every day. This means that certain parts of the body and certain muscles get used frequently, while other parts of the body and muscles rarely receive any attention. This creates imbalances in the body. The same principle can apply to our practice of sports, where we might overdevelop certain parts of the body at the expense of other parts. We need to move, dance, and stretch in different directions on a daily basis. The ancient tradition of yoga attends to many parts of the body. It is often forgotten that yoga belongs to a much wider tradition of mindfulness, meditation, diet, livelihood, and holistic lifestyle.

PRACTICE: YOGA

The great yogis would never endorse the use of Hatha Yoga isolated from a healthy lifestyle. The original meaning of *yoga* means to be yoked to or joined to a deep sense of something— life, truth, God— that is greater than our mortal existence. We practice yoga to learn what it means to live as a yogi in the concrete jungle of daily life.

There are several simple yoga exercises that will loosen up the body, open the cells, cultivate greater flexibility, and strengthen muscles. These exercises are not strenuous, and are practices that can be undertaken at home. However, to gain the full benefits from yoga practice, it is necessary to find a yoga teacher.

Try the following simple exercises, giving two or three minutes to each. Remember always to do them with relaxed breathing.

EXERCISE: PRACTICING YOGA

1 Stand with your feet close together. Roll your neck first in one direction and then in the other.

2 Raise the shoulders up to the ears, and then relax while lowering your shoulders. Squeeze the shoulder blades together and relax.

3 Raise your arms above your head and hook your thumbs together, breathing in and out through your stomach.

4 Allow both arms to hang down, fingers pointing to the toes, and stretch your back, without forcing it.

5 Straighten your arms, and point your fingers to the ceiling. Lead your body to the left slowly to stretch the right side. Repeat, leading your body to the right slowly to stretch the left side.

6 Lie on your back with your feet close together. Lift both feet off the ground, hold for a few seconds, and release.

7 Lie on your back and bend your knees. Place your arms around your shins, and lift the knees and head, to come close to each other.

Do the next part of the exercise lifting and bending your left leg first. When you have completed the exercise, place your arms around your shins, and lift your knees and head, to come close to each other. Then lift and bend your right leg in the same way.
8 Lie on your stomach and lift the left leg straight off the ground separately and then the other leg.

9 Stand straight and extend your arms straight out ahead of you. Bend your knees.
10 Very slowly, moment to moment extend your arms straight out from your shoulders and slowly raise your arms until your fingertips point to the sky. Then, with straight arms, lower them down, bending your back slowly until your fingertips point to the toes. Allow your body to hang down for several seconds without forcing your back to bend further. Then slowly raise your arms, straighten your back, and let your arms hang down at the side of your body with your chest expanding. Breathe mindfully.

Take a rest. Lie down in the horizontal posture with your arms at the side and your feet just a couple of inches apart. Be still. Breathe gently. Rest for at least five to ten minutes.

EXERCISE: ACHIEVING CALMNESS

Develop practices for a calm relationship to the body so that when you are ill the mind is not putting pressure on the body to get well.
Mindfulness of breathing, scanning the attention from head to toes (see earlier exercises), sitting or lying in complete stillness help to acknowledge harmony of mind with body.
If there is pain in the body, quietly but firmly turn the attention to the area of pain. Explore it from the outer edges to the very center.
Take notice and appreciate all the locations where there isn't pain.

reLationsHips anD minDfuLness

Couples

One or two generations ago, couples relied on the support of their marriage vows to ensure a long-term commitment to their relationship. Not any longer. Half the marriages in any capital city will end in divorce. We have to prepare for change whether we like it or not.

The transition from partnership to friendship, whether after a long-term or short-term relationship, is a major challenge. It is not unusual at the end of a relationship for one partner to experience a period of mourning rather similar to that following the death of a loved one. In other cases, a relationship that has dissolved can leave the two people as intractable enemies or smoldering in silent resentment. It takes a depth of maturity, kindness, and an ability to let go to achieve a successful transition to friendship.

On the face of it, it seems a pity that two people can fall in love with each other, or feel strongly attracted to each other, so much so that they embark upon a relationship, only to withdraw from each other later. Partners can start their relationship in heaven and finish up in hell. There are perhaps three important features that contribute to the ending of a relationship.

1 LOSS OF TRUST
Many of us experience vulnerability if our partner flirts with or spends a lot of time with somebody else. Mistrust, fear, and doubts will have an effect on communication, and sometimes one partner will try to exert control over the other to ensure the relationship stays together. This pressure may succeed initially, but often brings about a lingering resentment that can result in arguments. The loss of trust may spring

entirely from an imagination riddled with fear, or from accurate perceptions, or both. If one partner has been having an affair, he or she may return to the relationship after the affair has ended. Direct knowledge of the affair can have a devastating impact on the other partner. We often say that time heals. It can help, providing there is a willingness not to cling to the past in any way. Then there is the possibility of moving forward. Both partners need to reflect honestly on the lessons to be learned from past behavior that triggered anguish and suffering.

2 GROWTH OF DISSATISFACTION

Dissatisfaction is insidious. Like water torture, it increases as a pressure drop by drop until it bursts the form of the relationship. Sometimes one partner constantly points out to the other what he or she dislikes about the other—whether it be speech, manner of dress, division of household tasks, financial concerns, or attitude. These comments can gradually corrupt and destroy a relationship.

3 LACK OF ADVENTURE

When one person in a relationship yearns for change, excitement, and to do new things, while the other resists change, frustration can result. We need to use our

imagination and develop the capacity to triumph over routine, otherwise a certain deadness fills the heart of a relationship.

The end of a relationship can be utterly unexpected and come without any warning signs. When this happens, it is helpful to ask yourself the following questions and remind yourself that when one door closes, a new one can open:

1 What would be three good reasons for me to have ended the relationship?
2 What do I need to accept?
3 What fresh opportunities will open in my life?

Sometimes, a regular spiritual practice such as prayer, chanting, devotion, or meditation seems an inadequate method to deal with loss. We feel utterly unable to focus our mind in such ways when confronted with our loss. We feel unable to connect with any kind of specific spiritual practice, and feel overwhelmed by abrupt and unwelcome changes in our life. We may need to explore other ways to change the state of turmoil we find ourselves in—there is no single method that can deal with all kinds of suffering.

Although we may take the opportunity to speak with a close friend or a trusted family member, their counsel may only provide temporary relief from the heartache. It isn't easy to attend directly to an emotionally difficult matter. Dance, movement, yoga, long walks, exposure to nature, singing, writing, deep breathing, as well as discussion with another individual or group, help to break up and dissolve the hardship of unwanted change. We also need to be reminded to hang in there until inner peace comes.

It is a hard task to cope with a sweeping range of emotions such as sadness, anger, and feelings of failure, and to understand why a person has suddenly withdrawn from our life. Honest questions can help. Our answers may seem abstract initially, but they can shed light on the pain of the situation.

Family Relationships

It seems somewhat ironic that members of family, linked through blood and personal history, often experience so much tension and fierce disagreement. We can treat family members far worse than anybody else we know. They are expected to tolerate our verbal abuse, entrenched views, and insensitivity—behavior that we would not expect anybody else to accept.

Issues of change and conflict frequently occur between family members. Without realizing it, our feuds can spill over into other areas of life, impacting on friends and work colleagues. We forget that the shadow of bad feelings distorts and colors numerous other perceptions, often without our realizing it. If we cannot resolve family tensions, we have little chance of finding resolution with others. At times, we convince ourselves that resolution of a conflict depends upon the cooperation of the other person. To some extent, this is true. However, this conviction is often used as a rationale to justify remaining stuck in our position rather than doing everything possible to resolve the situation. What is needed is love, sacrifice, and generosity of spirit. Even if other family members remain frozen in their view, it does not justify our clinging to a position of conflict.

Mindfulness practice will help us to develop the discipline of accepting what we don't like in somebody else. We have to learn to accept the totality of a person—we can't just respond to features of the personality of which we approve, and condemn those we don't like. The true nature of a human being stands beyond likes and dislikes. If we are to understand a person, this means embracing the ugly side that can wind us up so quickly. Once we have raised our voice in an argument, we have lost that argument. We would like life to be easy, but it isn't. We have to accept this and endeavor on all occasions to respond as well as we can to our difficulties with each other.

We have much more in common than we realize. Let us never forget this so that we abide intimately with each other in this vast web of existence.

EXERCISE: REFLECTING ON RELATIONSHIPS

If your relationship has ended, make a daily resolve to act wisely.

Be watchful of the tendency toward blame, either of yourself or another.

Make time to reflect afterward on any conversation you may have had about the end of the relationship.

Does it show clarity or reactivity? Are you clinging to the past or is there light at the end of the tunnel?

EXERCISE: OVERCOMING SORROW

If you are experiencing sorrow or grief, remind yourself that this experience is temporary. Be alert to the fact that these strong emotions can feed all manner of thoughts that become a loop to reify intense emotions.

Keep your body straight and upright as much as possible, with your eyes open. A straight back helps to keep the energy flowing evenly to protect us from getting overwhelmed with sorrow. When the head and body slumps we can fall into despair.

Stay outdoors as much as possible, preferably in a park or in the countryside.

Let light, space, and color enter your inner life.

Share your experiences with a good friend. Take notice of wise advice.

making changes

The ancient teachings about the power of mindfulness take us closer not only to our everyday experiences, but also to ourselves. This practice requires a real interest in bringing mindfulness to bear on the most ordinary actions, instead of allowing the force of habit to rule our consciousness.

We could begin with the most simple and familiar of all acts, namely making a cup of tea. Mindfulness might encourage us to reflect on the tea we use—for example organic, caffeine-free, or herbal tea—or the milk—organic or skim. Do we need milk or sugar? Do we sip the tea mindfully, taking our time to acknowledge the full taste of the tea? Upon finishing the cup of tea, we can practice to give equal mindfulness to the washing and drying of the cup. Through your own experience you can see what a difference it makes when you increase the quality of attention to such a simple thing as having a cup of tea.

In the silent and conscientious process of making ourselves a cup of tea, there is a sense about the experience that transforms it into something that we might be bold enough to regard as spiritual or sacred. Not suprisingly, there is a tradition in Zen Buddhism devoted to the art of making and drinking a cup of tea. With this in mind, imagine the difference it would make if we totally dedicated a whole day to such a quality of mindfulness. The Buddha said it is better to live a wise and mindful life for one day than to live a hundred years in an unwise and unmindful way.

With sustained mindfulness, our relationship to what we see, hear, smell, taste, and touch changes. It enlivens our interest as we move from one situation to the next, taking real notice of what we do as well as observing our intentions and attitudes toward what we do. The introduction of mindfulness as a feature of and a commitment in our daily life will mark a turning point in our existence, opening up the doorway to fresh ways of understanding our participation in the world.

Mindfulness should not be regarded as a means for exercising greater control over our lives, though it can also be helpful in this way. Some people are naturally mindful—their homes are very tidy, and they are careful about the way they dress, work, or handle situations. These personality traits show a conscientious way of life. Others become obsessive through clinging to appearances, order, and strict timetables. The obsessive personality becomes agitated when situations get out of his or her control.

Growing numbers of people are searching for deeper values beyond conventional secular culture with its emphasis on career, income, and immersion in the pursuit of pleasure. For those who want to explore the depths of spiritual experiences, the so-called "real world" reveals only a small framework of existence. What truly matters lies outside this value system rather than within it.

The practice of mindfulness reveals a great deal about what goes on within ourselves. It makes what has become unconscious much more conscious. It is this direct exposure to inner material that has been neglected, sometimes for years, that makes

clear to us what we have to face up to and what we have to change. As time goes by, we begin to realize the personal, social, and political significance of mindfulness.

From the standpoint of the spiritual life, it is a human duty to work on ourselves, to apply *upaya* (from the Sanskrit, meaning "skillful means"). For all of us, without exception, there are aspects of our lives that have to change. Our lives are in constant change, constant flux. Every moment is a transition to another moment. Nothing stands still. We are exposed to impermanence and change through every perception, state of mind, and thought. Part of spiritual practice is learning to live at peace with changes, whether we initiate them or they come to us.

We need to develop the determination to make changes so that we stop ignoring unhealthy or unwholesome features, whether inward or outward, that are creating difficulties for us as well as making an impact upon others. We have to examine our tendencies of mind, be willing to name areas that deserve attention, and start to change them. It is the practice of transforming what the Buddha refers to as the "three poisons of the mind," namely greed, hate, and delusion.

Greed

We associate greed with going after more than we need. This includes everything with regard to any of the five senses. Halting greed is a statement of spiritual awareness. It is learning to see the world in fresh ways, rather than through the eyes of desire. You only have to be in the countryside and look at the vast panorama of light and color in the sky and on the earth to realize how much this expanse nourishes our being. We can never own all of that. We can buy a large mansion with lots of land, but it shrinks to insignificance when compared with the great expanse of existence that is before our eyes.

With our ears, we experience the sounds of nature, whether it is the bird singing its love song, or the breezes gently rustling in the trees. We can turn our awareness to the space between the sounds and the space that surrounds the sounds as the sound vibrations reach our ears. We can also sense this space between the objects that we see with our eyes. Stillness and silence coexist with movement and sound. When we demand nothing from this world, it reveals to us an extraordinary dimension of wonder that our heart responds to with effortless ease. Shown through desire and greed, egotism inhibits the ability of our consciousness to open itself up. We practice to be content with what we have. It is the sign of inner wealth.

Hate

Another limiting, narrow, and restricted pattern of mind is hate—and in its subtle forms, anger, agitation, and negativity—which corrupts the inner life and spills outward in destructive ways. We often don't realize how small our mind has become until we get caught up in our wrath over something or someone, as if our sanctimonious and self-righteous opinions really matter.

Our petty views not only impress upon us our own limitations and lack of wisdom, but also cause distress to or reaction from others, personally, socially, and internationally. We give support to hatred when we support the oppressive and violent policies of our governments and military leaders. We have a way of masking this hatred through cultured and sophisticated forms of language and the application of cold reason to our hardened views. The result is still terror and pain to people, animals, and the environment.

If we seek to cause harm to others, whether through unleashing a torrent of words or with detached and ruthless comments used to maximize the pain of another, we need to examine why. We may speak with someone face to face, or communicate through letters and e-mails, or through a third person. We may try to justify our outbursts, or later feel remorse and shock at what came out of our mind. In either case, we need to change.

Again, we ask ourselves in what ways we can look at a situation outside our usual conditioned reactivity. We have to dig deep into ourselves to come up with a different way of understanding. That might take the support of another to change the condition of our inner life. When things go wrong for us, when we cannot get our own way, it is all too easy to feel embittered at the outcome. Do we honestly believe that everything has to work according to our will? Doesn't this kind of reactivity ignore the reality of life?

If we are to express our nobility as human beings and transform our inner life so that we gain clear insights into what impacts upon our lives, we must be committed to change. There is never any guarantee that communication will flow well, that both parties will be satisfied, or that there will be peace of mind after a meeting. It is to be hoped that we can place hand on heart at the end of a difficult meeting and say to ourselves that we endeavored to respond wisely and factually rather than with negativity and resentment.

Delusion

Delusion is the third "poison of the mind" and refers to a wide range of states of mind, including fear, rejection, egotism, arrogance, and beliefs that uphold the ego of "I," "me," and "my." Delusion acts like a cloud over consciousness, and we find ourselves looking at the world through these distortions. We do not realize that these unhealthy states of mind make up a delusion. We have come to believe that our distorted perceptions mirror reality.

Upholding and cherishing our standpoints, we forget to treat them as views and opinions and look at them as statements of absolute truth. As some of these clouds that obscure the natural sunlight of consciousness fade away, we realize the degree to which clinging and grasping shape our view of existence. We can only accept our perception of events at the expense of somebody else's. Calm and insight help to dissolve greed, hate, and delusion so that we can express generosity, kindness, and clarity instead.

When we stop clinging to "I," "me," and "my," we can give support to love and wisdom and give up notions of ownership and control. This understanding shows us that nothing belongs to us and, at the deepest level of things, we have nothing and own nothing. There is simply the moment-to-moment connection with what is happening here and now. Kahil Gibran, the Lebanese poet, penned one of the most poetic descriptions of this nonpossessive kind of understanding in his book *The Prophet*, where he wrote an exquisite piece about our relationship to children.

CHILDREN

Your children are not your children.
They are the sons and daughters of
life longing for itself.
They come through you not from you.
And though they are with you yet
they belong not to you.
You may give them your love but
not your thoughts
For they have their own thoughts
You may house their bodies but not their souls…
You may strive to be like them, but seek not to make them like you.
For life goes not backward nor tarries with yesterday.
You are the bows from which your children as living arrows are sent forth.

from *The Prophet*
KAHIL GIBRAN [2]

Children are truly living statements of wonder and deserve our greatest love and respect, but they are not our possessions, nor should we try to make our children in our image. All children in the world deserve to be bombarded with love—morning, noon, and night—because they give to us as much, if not more, than we could ever offer to them.

Kahil Gibran reminds us in an extraordinarily poetic way that our children are not our own. Wisdom distinguishes between respect and support, control and domination, especially when we know deep down in ourselves that our children belong to the universe, and are not our possessions. For it is in our belief that we "possess" our children that we try to fashion them to our likeness, instill into them our prejudices, and try to make them clones of ourselves. We often think we know what is best for them, and frequently we don't. What is best for children is love, helpful guidelines, and giving them the freedom to be themselves. This same bare truth applies to adults who also wish to be treated with love and respect. Everything belongs to life, to the nature of things, to God, not to ourselves. Let us reflect on this vital understanding. Let us meditate on this to free our minds and to share that freedom and understanding as well. Then we bring wisdom to every relationship and every area of our lives. Then true love rules the heart. When we tackle the forces of greed, hate, and delusion, within or without, and practice to make changes in our conditioned perceptions and open our hearts to a greater vision, we enhance our lives and provide a service to life itself.

EXERCISE: MEDITATING ON CHANGE

Meditate on change, on impermanence. Be mindful of all the changes that take place during the day—inwardly and outwardly. Hold onto none of them to remain as open as possible to all new experiences.

Remember that at the closing of one door another one opens. Purposefully cultivate the attitude of wise connection with moment-to-moment change.

If you feel stuck or trapped, remind yourself that this feeling and view will change.

EXERCISE: DEALING WITH THE EGO

Reflect on "I," "me," and "my" from the aspect of whether it is a simple use of language or charged with ego. The ego shows itself most noticeably in unhealthy states of mind such as greed, anger, delusion, fear, pride, and so on. Select one pattern of mind and make it a practice to work with it for its transformation.

experiencing oneness

Cogito, Ergo Sum

Mindfulness encourages deep experiences beyond the divisive field of thought so that we realize our intimacy with all things. Deep changes come to our life through a different sense of things when the belief in "self" and "other" loses its substance.

At first glance, it might seem peculiar in a book on mindfulness to refer to René Descartes, the seventeenth-century philosopher, regarded as one of the most

important influences upon Western thought in the last three hundred years. As a young man, Descartes realized the significance of scientific knowledge based on mathematics. He believed that science would establish objective truth as being self-evident. He held the view that there was a certainty in scientific knowledge

not found in other views of reality. He relied upon the principles of mathematics to prove his point, holding tightly to the belief that scientists can deduce the phenomena of nature through the various branches of mathematics. He also arrived at arguably the most famous philosophical statement in the Western world: *Cogito, ergo sum*, meaning "I think, therefore I am." Descartes insisted that though we must be willing to doubt everything, we cannot doubt that we think. From this conclusion, he proceeded to provide a methodology for scientists to think through their scientific investigations and conclusions.

Mindfulness practice also encourages the willingness to doubt everything without exception, including the statement *Cogito, ergo sum*. It endorses a quiet determination to experience a mindful state of not knowing, an innocence, and a humility, so that the truths of life reveal themselves. This means turning *Cogito, ergo sum* into a question: "I think, therefore I am?" or "I think, therefore I am what?"

The great teachers of mindfulness practice in the East, particularly in the Buddhist tradition, strongly emphasize the questioning of our existence. The questions "Who am I? What am I? Am I?" are regarded as the toughest of all spiritual contemplations—the investigation into the nature of the self has the power to blow apart all of the assumptions and images under which we live. This kind of mindfulness practice, with the question "Who am I?" at its center, points to the essence of spiritual realization. The purpose behind the inquiry is to wake up. When we truly wake up, our old life and identity wrapped up in conventional existence ends—it is as if we have been living in a dream.

Descartes' *Cogito, ergo sum* has had a threefold impact on Western consciousness:

1 It gives authority to the supremacy of thought. Thought then becomes the instrument with which we define the world through scientific analysis.

2 It places thought in a unique category, cut off from the body, the emotions, and the rest of the world. Thought is granted an exclusive and objective role in defining the real world.

3 It relies upon thought to isolate and pick out features of phenomena such as the body, energy, or matter, to establish a scientific standpoint. It inevitably leads to a reductionist view of existence.

Today's World

Understandably impressed with scientific achievement, we have developed a questionable degree of confidence in the army of scientists attempting to resolve the various crises that we face in our lives. Television news programs, documentaries, and newspaper articles often tell us about the latest scientific breakthrough and offer glimpses of the brave, new world, yet the problems of humanity and the environment still seem greater than the long list of scientific achievements designed to resolve them.

Our mindfulness practice reminds us to engage in full participation in the adventure of existence, rather than adopting the detached, clinical view of the scientist, who has persuaded him- or herself that they know reality. We do not have to treat the world as a complex machine determined by a range of mathematical laws. We do not have to subscribe to the viewpoint that accompanies scientific beliefs that the world exists for our benefit, once we have broken down elemental matter and reconstituted it in our laboratories, whether in a constructive way (such as advancements in health care) or in a destructive way (such as the production of sophisticated weapons).

Mindfulness practice strongly doubts the view that we exist in order to engineer the world to our satisfaction and to exploit its resources to our advantage. Descartes may well have changed his worldview if he had witnessed the explosive rise of the Industrial Revolution, underpinned by scientific research, and its cost to global life.

We delude ourselves if we imagine that we can master the world. It is in this respect that mindfulness has a radical aspect.

Many practitioners of mindfulness, including countless Buddhists, forget the importance of deep inquiry as a feature of mindfulness. Without the questioning mind, the practice becomes viewed as a means to living a calm, stress-free life, with an air of inner peace about our demeanor. There is certainly much virtue in such a way of being, but we must regard inner well-being only as a major step toward radical realizations, so that we are not afraid to go beyond our thought-driven view of existence.

Mindfulness explores the full range of human experience in everyday life. A genuine inquiry with a practical methodology takes a circumspect view of fixing reality into any kind of framework—scientific, philosophical, or religious. This may all seem abstract and theoretical to many readers, but mindfulness practices require a willingness to change our worldview. The main point to remember is the value of a holistic view of life where a sense of participation, rather than domination and ownership, takes priority.

Views about reality get passed down from one generation to the next. We practice mindfulness to overcome materialistic views of existence with desire for ownership as our priority. Embedded deep in our mind, we have come to believe that living in the real world means supporting scientific materialism and economic development as the only view that matters. Mindful living expresses care, concern, and respect for people and the environment.

Today we find ourselves living in a culture that sustains the separation of the mind, the body, and the world, while reducing everything to subatomic particles and DNA as the basis of reality. In the space of a generation, there is an increasingly held view that interdependence, the great web of interconnection, reflects more accurately the way things are. Mindfulness practice establishes the web of interconnection as central to our understanding of the nature of reality. With that as our basis, we consider this connection in all our major dealings with the world. It may not be too long before the worldview of Descartes becomes a view belonging to the second millennium. Instead we will experience reality through the web of interdependency.

I fly regularly to different parts of the world to give teachings on meditation and spiritual enlightenment. In a single flight from London to New York, as a passenger I must accept responsibility for the aircraft's emissions that are as much as from the average use of a car (I don't own one) for a year. In my public talks, I sometimes remind listeners of this uncomfortable fact. I believe my visit to another country to teach is justified, provided that my teachings contribute directly and immediately to people committing themselves to a more moderate lifestyle as an ethical value in the practice of mindfulness.

Like Descartes, we often adopt the view of the separation of mind from matter but we have other experiences that refute that standpoint. Let us take a simple example. You are spending a day outdoors, perhaps walking in the mountains, spending time by the sea, observing a beautiful sunset, or idly watching a river from a bridge. You experience a deep sense of oneness, of unity, a pervasive and harmonious uninterrupted presence

of nature that is free from any division. This unshakable dimension dissolves divisions, including the belief that "this is me in this spot and what is out there is not me." Suddenly, and rather unexpectedly, all scientific and religious standpoints seem irrelevant in such an experience. It is not that these experiences are particularly rare or encountered only by mystics. The chances are that many readers have experienced spontaneously, in meditation, or in a sudden change of consciousness and energy, this unitive sense about life. It is an authentic experience revealing an extraordinary oneness of existence that dissolves the assertion of the division of mind and matter.

If thoughts dismiss this quality of experience, we are likely to go back to the Cartesian view of self and the world with science as the only means to know reality. One deep experience of oneness can make a considerable difference to our attitude toward life and our intentions in this vast field of interconnection. We realize how interdependent all things are and the role we have within this interdependency. The common view held during the second millennium, that we have the inalienable right to control the earth purely for our benefit and convenience, becomes redundant.

If we experience and trust in a unitive experience that offers a different way of looking at reality, then it will influence how we feel, speak, and act in this world. In this perception and realization, we will be mindful of the ways that we contribute to expressing an interconnection with life, and the ways that we ignore it. We will then come to know that in the reality of things, we abide in a remarkable global network of life, which involves humans, animals, and the environment all interacting and mutually supporting each other. This vision of existence deserves our care and attention.

At first glance, it would seem self-evident that we exist as our "self" and that all else is not our "self." Descartes surely would not argue with that. We examine ourselves from head to toes, assuming that body, mind, and speech make up who we are: "This is me. This is who I am. This is my self." Then we say that what is outside of us is clearly and obviously not our "self"—namely the world around us. Life is then divided into a duality called "me" and "not me." Under the influence of this seemingly self-evident perception, we conduct our lives, and act out our belief in *Cogito, ergo sum.* If this basis for reality is ultimately false, then it means that our lives have become false as a consequence. Is it any wonder that we have become so confused, fearful, and self-centered?

We experience what influences us, and we also experience that we influence what is around us. Sometimes our experiences are as a result of the choices that we make. Sometimes the world impacts upon us, and we have no choice. Sometimes we influence the immediate world intentionally, and sometimes we influence it unintentionally. What if ultimately these views of existence are not true? What if they are a dream? What if the saints and sages past and present are right? What if millions of people are living in the same dream but have come to think of it as the only reality? What would burst the bubble? Would we want it to burst? Do we want to wake up?

The Present

All the mindfulness practices in this book, and similar spiritual texts, point us in this direction of waking up. In our abiding interest to come to see things clearly, rather

than adopting the prevailing views in science or education, we need to learn to cultivate a quiet, calm, and still mind on a daily basis, free from distractions. We need to allow ourselves to settle into the present moment, just for itself. In this sublime refinement, there is a fusion, a sense of wholeness, that brings its own understanding of reality. There is no permanence or everlasting continuity in this experience, but it keeps renewing itself through conscious contact with the adventure of existence.

In the experience of such awareness and presence, there is a sense that the real truth of life is at hand, unfiltered by viewpoints, memories, or projections. Our discoveries cannot become compressed into a mathematical formula or an equation. Such an awareness has an enlightening element to it. True reality is indivisible. It cannot be broken down or fitted into a system of thought. It treats our beliefs and views as contextual rather than absolute. There is a timeless knowing that transcends cultural conditioning and the current views and values of society.

We are blessed with a realization that ultimately there is no big difference between yesterday, today, and tomorrow. As the mind empties itself of its contents, it allows realizations to open our consciousness out.

In such experiences, we lose our infatuation with time, with things and events, past, present, and future. This enables us to feel an extraordinary sense of the vast, unfolding process of life, the great sweep of existence that fills us up and nourishes our entire being. The systematic effort to acquire as many pleasures as possible can never serve as a substitute for such revelations. In our realization of the undivided fullness of things, our problems shrink away, leaving a contentment, joy, and love free from regret or fear of the future.

The true reality of things is not as we usually think it to be. There is integrity in the willingness to allow ourselves to have doubts about our repetitive thoughts. As human beings, we have a remarkable potential to realize the fullness of things that remain unbroken and untarnished.

EXERCISE: EXPERIENCING NATURE

Go out into nature with the intention of exploring and experiencing the unity of life. Be aware of the sky, earth, trees, grass, and flowers, and the whole sense of life. Feel your participation in the unfolding process of life and sense the whole web of existence as it interacts.

Make this a regular commitment so that you feel more at home with the events of daily life and the intimate expanse of nature.

EXERCISE: EXPERIENCING ONENESS

If you have any experiences of the sense of oneness and unity of all life, then make time to reflect on their value.

- Why are such experiences important?
- What priorities do they bring to your life?
- What does the experience of oneness tell you about fragmentation and divisive experiences?
- What embraces both separateness and unity?

3: mindfulness of inner life

cultivating wise intention

The surgeon working in the operating room on a major operation, and the burglar stealthily going from room to room, have something in common. Both show an extraordinary degree of mindfulness from one moment to the next. Both remain completely absorbed in their work. What separates the surgeon and the burglar is the intention—and that intention makes all the difference, even though in both cases the quality of focused attention is extraordinarily high. The burglar generates suffering that an insurance policy cannot redress. The surgeon, on the other hand, works to relieve suffering for a patient.

Authentic mindfulness takes into consideration the intentions behind our actions. Intentions matter as much as mindfulness. Together they have the power to transform our lives. Our intentions act as a governing force behind our actions. Even if we make mistakes and the results do not work out the way we want, we can take note of our intentions. If we know deep in our heart that our intentions are wholesome, then we should take comfort in this knowledge.

If we apply right intention to right mindfulness, we develop a resource that enables us to be truly present to situations in a clear and caring way. Both intention and mindfulness are factors in the Buddha's Noble Eightfold Path to an enlightened life. The other factors are right understanding, right speech, right action, right livelihood, right effort, and right meditation. To realize fulfillment in life, we give attention to all eight factors. We have the opportunity to open up to a whole new vista of existence that eludes us in many ways through distorted and habitual states of mind. That may mean making a firm intention to opening up our horizons through a more conscious life.

In the Buddhist tradition, intention or motivation acts as an essential principle behind whatever we do or want to do, whether in terms of work, study, leisure, relationships, or spiritual exploration. If we remain aware of our intentions, we will notice if they change, whether for better or worse. It is all too easy to start with a wholesome motivation in a personal endeavor, such as the intention to give support to others, and end being motivated by the ego boost our actions bring.

Right intention is a core element in spiritual life but intentions alone are not enough. We can be full of good intentions but never follow up on them. Right intention leads to skillful action. From a spiritual perspective, it means that such an intention needs to be followed up with skillful means. In one discourse, the Buddha said that we have the potential to realize full liberation if we practice mindfulness, not for seven years or even seven months, but if we practice wholeheartedly for seven days. That means having a clear intention to awaken and stay awake.

It would certainly seem worthwhile to examine our intentions, to see whether we regard them as wholesome, unwholesome, or neither. Our feelings and emotions easily have a major impact on our intentions. If we feel happy and loving, we will probably express much kindness and generosity. If we feel hurt or unhappy, we may want to hurt another through revenge, withdrawal, or blame. We need to be very honest with ourselves at such times, and acknowledge the intentions that inform what we say or do. Remember that our intentions not only have an impact on the lives of others, but also on ourselves.

We ought to adopt a pragmatic position. Our unhealthy intentions will perpetuate our unhappiness if we desire to hurt another or others for what they have done or intended to do to us. We have to be honest. Do I want to sink to their level if I have been exploited? Alternatively, can I use a healthy intention to rise above the situation? This is the greatest challenge when we pass through a tense situation, even a short-lived one. For example, when driving along a busy road and another driver cuts in front, nearly causing an accident, we might swear at the driver and wave our fists in anger. The impatience of the other driver triggers our anger. If we grasp onto our reaction, we might find ourselves trying to get past the driver to upset him. This is road rage. It is not only dangerous, but springs from an inability to look at our state of mind to catch the intention. Clear mindfulness of our intentions makes the whole manner of our activities different. Instead of reactivity, we approach a difficult situation with full alertness to our subsequent motivation. We endeavor to stay true to acting wisely when under threat. None would say this is easy. Situations will test our patience and equanimity. That is a guarantee.

Mindfulness, along with clear comprehension, dissolves our latent tendencies to indulge in daydreams and fantasies. It is all too human to get lost in such states of mind, sometimes as a way to avoid the present moment. Buddhist teachings have always regarded such states of mind as belonging to a dream world that consciousness finds itself immersed in as if it were reality. One of the clear functions of mindfulness is to break up these patterns sufficiently so that we genuinely wake up to the immediacy of reality. Mindfulness unlocks the door. The clear intention to stay present is the key. There is much to appreciate in the here and now, much to realize and much to wake up to in the present moment. The here and now has the power to transform our lives.

As a major resource for a transformed life, the teachings of mindfulness seem deceptively simple. If you say to yourself or others, "I am a mindful person," then the chances are that you have not truly entered the depths of mindful living and total attention to the here and now. Commitment to mindfulness and wise intention embraces such concurrent factors as wise speech, skillful effort, right action, and depths of meditation. You can only start in this moment.

You might be tempted to tell yourself that you will start a serious mindfulness practice tomorrow. That would be a postponement that gives license to living in the dream world longer than necessary. This moment counts. This is the moment where you have exposure to the presence of life. In reality, there is no tomorrow. There is no other time or place to turn to. Is there any real choice between staying fully awake to this moment and living out of touch, often dull, unhappy, and confused? Who would choose the latter? It may be worthwhile to reflect regularly on the value of staying present to keep our intention strong so that we abide with a clear and purposeful mind amid the ebb and flow of circumstances.

At times we certainly need to strengthen our intention, to give it extra focus, energy, and consciousness, so it has a resolve to it. We need to ask ourselves whether we have a genuine depth of intention to overcome problems. We need resolve. In some cases, this resolve needs to be strong from the time that we wake up in the morning. There is little point in leaving reminders on the refrigerator door or stuck on the kitchen wall. We all know how quickly we can even forget their existence so that nothing really happens. We have to remind ourselves inwardly to keep our resolve about something that matters to us.

Resolve

A genuine sense of resolve comes out of the heart. We have to be consciously determined to carry something through. First, we recognize the problem, then we cultivate the intention to make a daily resolve to overcome it, and then we carry it through. We must apply these three principles every day, on the easy days, as well as during those times when we are dealing directly with, say, a nicotine addiction. We have to remember that the determination to overcome a problem must be stronger than the habitual determination to feed the addiction.

At times, this process of making significant changes goes from effort to effortlessness, as our mind understands the wisdom of what we are doing. Yet this clear sign of firm progress along the path toward inner change easily leads into complacency. We can delude ourselves into thinking we have put the addiction behind us. Let us never underestimate the latent forces within that propel us back into the habit. The password is constant vigilance. As we sustain our vigilance, we will experience a genuine difference and a realization that this difference will bring about an appreciation for what we have achieved and what we have overcome. As we notice this inner development, we also feel correspondingly that we are putting behind us the problem itself. Once that shift has been completely made, we feel content. The habit of smoking has gone. We have given ourselves several extra years of life. Our cells can renew themselves now that they are free from attack from nicotine and thousands of chemicals. We save hundreds of dollars every year. We turn our back on the merciless tobacco industry and we help to protect others from polluted air, while land can be used to grow food instead of tobacco plants for cancer cultivated for human addiction. It is a victory for common sense and for awareness, thanks to a firm resolution as the treatment.

It would appear that there is an underlying intention behind everything we do. It isn't always easy to know what our intention is. For wise intention we must be ruthlessly honest with ourselves. It requires clearness about our state of mind and the feelings that influence our intention. Self-honesty is an unshakable principle for wise intention. As an integral key to wise intention, self-honesty forces us to examine

ourselves before we act. If we ignore the importance of honesty, we are likely to disguise our intention, and this will deceive others as well as ourselves.

Let us really experience our connection with what is, so that we bring the full force of mindfulness to the reality of what is going on. Let us live an authentic existence and remain utterly honest about our intentions and motives. Let us be mindful. Be aware. Be conscious. Stay awake.

EXERCISE: MAKING INTENTIONS

Make a firm intention, motivation, or resolution to stay present and connected with as many moments as possible.
Make the intention to stay calm and conscious throughout the whole day.
Practice to relax into every situation, even if things are not going as you would wish. Don't neglect mindfulness of breathing as a basic aid.
Ask yourself whether there is any area of your life where you need to make the intention healthy and wholesome.
Make that intention until it is well established within.

EXERCISE: FOCUSING ON PRIORITIES

Take one important area of your life and write down your primary intentions in that area. Be totally honest. Are you satisfied with these intentions? Do you want to change them?
If you make changes in your intentions, be clear about them and remind yourself of them.
Remember that wisdom includes the application of skillful intention for the benefit of yourself and others.

attending to Loneliness

Loneliness is a major social issue that makes people vulnerable to a wide number of other painful states of mind. Some reports indicate that in various capital cities in Europe more than fifty percent of the population live alone. For some, this choice allows the individual to have a certain degree of control over the home environment. Others would prefer to live with another person, but find themselves living alone because of a separation, divorce, bereavement, or failure to meet someone to share their home with. There are single parents as well who would dearly love to share their lives with others, but rarely find the opportunity to meet someone with whom to develop such a committed closeness.

Many people appreciate living alone; they have a number of friends and relatives who they can call upon, and they move in a social circle of people who may also choose to live alone. There is an increasing number of people in relationships, whether short- or long-term, who prefer to live separately rather than together. They may even feel that their relationship is far more sustainable if they live apart rather than together. Such lifestyle choices can relieve many of the pressures that can accumulate when we share the same space with another person seven days a week.

Mindfulness in everyday life includes our relationship to ourselves, whether we live alone, with another, or with several others. It is not unusual for waves of unrest to pass through the mind, whatever our domestic circumstances. Sometimes people who live together yearn for an opportunity to be alone; others who live alone find themselves envying those couples who have an ongoing relationship, particularly when it appears harmonious and well integrated.

One of the greatest challenges of mindful living for those who live alone, is the vulnerability to experiencing loneliness. It is quite possible to feel cut off and alienated, and unable to think of a single person to contact. The greater the desire for a social life or companionship, the greater the degree of loneliness. Such individuals may have all the social skills to create friendship with warm hearts and accommodating minds, yet find that their deeply wished-for companion or partner fails to materialize. This desire for closeness, perhaps for friendship, communication, or sexual intimacy with another, brings a kind of anguish and frustration, even self-blame. The evening can become the most difficult time of the day. The strength of this experience of loneliness can become very intense, and television programs, the radio, or food become a means to escape this distressingly difficult emotion.

Manifestation

The demon of loneliness manifests in a variety of ways, so we need to be mindful of the manifestation of the conditions for loneliness. Sometimes, loneliness is the fruit of a relationship that has ended. We have been in a close relationship, even if it has been difficult and painful. When it finishes, there is a loss of contact, of sharing of concerns, as well as struggles. The resulting loneliness often seems harder to deal with than the problems in the relationship.

It is often assumed that the one who makes the decision to end the relationship has the power, while the person on the receiving end of the decision is disempowered. However, the person who calls a halt to the relationship may feel the backlash from within themselves at a later date. Regrets, self-blame, and guilt can be unleashed into the mind, while the former partner may come to accept the decision, and

experience, after a while, relief at the opportunity to move on. Loneliness may haunt the lives of either person. There isn't an easy solution to this.

Loneliness also manifests in a yearning for contact with others, and a desire to be acknowledged and to be loved. Growing tired of our own company, we long for a close friend to share our life with, who will act as a pillar of support. Mindfulness of loneliness has to take into account a different kind of viewpoint. We have to dig deep within ourselves, as if we will never have contact with others again. We have to make friends with the here and now, and develop a capacity to love silence and stillness. When we feel lonely, what is taking place within is that the self and unpleasant feelings of separation have begun to fuse together, creating a sense of isolation. This can happen even when we are in the company of others. It isn't an easy task to acknowledge feelings of loneliness; we need to learn to stay with these experiences and not forget that they are waves of the isolated self that will come to pass.

Sometimes the evening can seem painfully long when the phone doesn't ring, and there is a reluctance to make a telephone call to anyone to stave off the loneliness. At such times, we need to ask ourselves:

- *Can we breathe through these feelings?*
- *Can we reflect daily on the benefits of living alone?*
- *Can we remind ourselves of the simple intimacies of what is around us?*
- *Can we engage in movement of our body to change the flow of energy so we don't concentrate on this terrible feeling of lacking a person with whom we can share our time?*

We can explore all these ways of making friends with ourselves, while keeping open the options for developing friendships with others. When loneliness gets a hold of us, we can easily find ourselves finding fault with or blaming others, particularly people we know. Such projections tell us more about ourselves than about the people we find fault with.

For some, the feeling of loneliness springs from fear of intimacy or simple lack of interest in the lives of others, and an unwillingness to take positive steps to be supportive and to act kindly toward others. We may need to take an honest look at ourselves. If we have spent years focused on self-interest, it will hardly inspire others to want to develop and maintain a close contact with us. We would have to change from self-interest to other interest, from self-concern to concern for others.

It is no easy task dealing with loneliness. It is one of those feelings where we know, without any doubt whatsoever, that we don't want to feel what we feel. Anything else seems better than enduring this emotion. It is the acknowledgment and utter acceptance of this feeling that starts the process of releasing its power over our emotional life. The greater the desire to escape this emotion, the greater the feeling of loneliness. Desire acts like wood on the fire of loneliness. The less the desire to escape it, then the greater the likelihood that this feeling of loneliness will lose its grip over our lives.

Resolution

To overcome our loneliness, we have to learn to appreciate ourselves, our immediate world, and what the here and now offers that we keep ignoring. Employing our eyes, ears, and reflective thinking, we can develop not only the quiet determination to have appropriate contact with others, but also the opportunity to develop contact with ourselves. Either we become lost in pity for ourselves, or we use our reasoning, imagination, and power of creative expression to make full use of the absence of the presence of others in our life. This is the crucial choice.

There is a delusional factor in loneliness with troublesome emotions. It is the persistence of a false belief—either about ourselves, or others, or both—in the reality of separation as the ultimate truth. When our desires for attention are thwarted, we compensate for this by indulging in unhappy states of mind. It is not an easy task to uplift the mind, to refuse to indulge in self-pity, and to remain quietly determined to lead an independent life, while remaining open to the possibilities of new friendships. If we can achieve this, then we have the opportunity to grow and develop. We are never too old for that. The resolution of loneliness is often both an inner and outer exploration. There is much to appreciate in life. It is not necessary that we have to find someone with whom to share these joys.

EXERCISE: OVERCOMING LONELINESS

Be very watchful about feeling sorry for yourself and then trying to fill the hole within through indulging in unhealthy habits.

Resolve to be active and creative.

Develop an appreciation of being alone.

Develop friendships without talking too much or too little.

Remember that quality in communication is preferable to quantity.

EXERCISE: CONNECTING WITH LIFE

Experience connection with plants, animals, and nature.

Keep a diary of everything new that you experience each day.

Write out your feelings and remember that many others share with you a similar experience of loneliness.

Be mindful of the times when this particular feeling is not present.

Acknowledge as fully as possible the times of connection with life and the here and now.

developing the power of friendship

The Buddha spent 45 years teaching in northern India to give support to the enlightenment of people wherever he went. He was frequently accompanied and attended by his close friend, Ananda, who took care of his personal needs and arranged various meetings with the people who came to see the Buddha. Ananda himself also took advantage of the Buddha's wisdom, asking the Buddha many questions. He once asked the Buddha if half of the reason for the spiritual life was friendship with others. The Buddha turned to Ananda, rebuking him mildly with the words, "Don't say that, Ananda. The whole of the spiritual life is for friendship." From this, it would appear that the Buddha elevated friendship to the highest status. However, we may feel that finding truth is the most important thing, or enlightenment, or finding God, or discovering liberation. How can friendship be in the same league as these discoveries of life?

Expanding the Heart

It is easy to forget that the core feature of Buddhist teachings concerns opening and expanding the heart until the Immeasurable is realized. In another language, it is the realization of being in the Kingdom of God. One of the clearest manifestations of that immeasurable realization shows itself in expanding our heart beyond all limitations. How easy it is for us to measure our friendship according to how others treat us, or how we treat them. The heart, free from limitations, sees the falseness of this constant classifying of people or a particular person into different categories of approval and disapproval.

So when the Buddha states that the whole of the spiritual life is for friendship, he truly means what he says. Is it possible to live in a world without enemies, without hatred, and without intolerance toward people we know and people we don't know? Is it possible to generate warmth and kindness toward everyone we meet and not express bitterness or violence about anyone, anywhere? Going beyond such limitations we are in fact close to the ultimate truth. In deep friendship, expansive love, and intimate connection, we know a life without limits or measurement. In the same way, the truth knows no limits. The Buddha has reminded Ananda that pervasive friendship is like true reality—limitless, vast, and expansive.

Obviously, it is an enormous undertaking to break open the shell of armor around the heart to the degree that our friendship toward all existence pervades in all directions without compromise. The many influences, healthy and unhealthy, that impact upon our lives from within and without make this task even harder. No human being can wake up in the morning and suddenly decide, "From now on, I am not going to have a bad thought about anybody. I am not going to utter a single word in anger. I am not going to do anything at all that hurts anybody else. I am going to live with a heart that abides unrestricted and reach out to all equally." It may be a sincere intention, but it has to be applied day in and day out until we finally break through and realize the enormous challenge we have undertaken. All genuine spiritual and religious teachings place emphasis on the heart, on clear acts of love and compassion that go beyond any kind of division of state or ethnic group.

As in other religions, it is easy to summarize this concept with a few lines such as, "Love your neighbor. Do good to those who hurt you. Forgive and forget." But how? As with other spiritual faiths, the Buddhist tradition recognizes the importance of the application of deep friendship toward all beings, including people, animals, and the environment. This friendship matters far more than the conversion of the individual to Buddhism. Many Buddhists regard labels such as "Buddhist" as having little importance or relevance on the global stage. What matters is our relationship to life and the expression of kindness.

Kindness

At the end of this chapter I have written a loving kindness meditation. As with some of the other meditations in the book, it is not necessary to follow the meditation precisely in terms of the formulation of words or prayer. It would be as worthwhile to write yourself a prayer of love that extends itself to everybody, near and far. You could memorize your meditation, which might consist of only one or two lines, with a view to saying them slowly, mindfully, and, most importantly, regularly, so that they gain the strength to enter our perception and communications. For example, Buddhists will often say at the end of a meditation or letter, "Sabbe Satta Sukhita Hontu." The words translate as, "May All Beings Be Happy." A regular meditation for friendship and loving kindness serves as the first step in the important process of expanding the heart beyond its usual capabilities.

We may think that we have a great deal of fear and anger to work on in ourselves that is obstructing the free flow of kindness. Through developing the power of kindness, we can deconstruct the forces of fear and anger so that they have little grip on our existence. Once we have convinced the heart and mind really to develop kindness and friendship, and we start truly putting it into practice, an inner power that develops that becomes fearless. This friendship expresses itself through the way we think, what we say, and what we do. Extending our vigilance to these three areas, we then have the capacity to become a single channel through which the kindness flows. Like a wind tunnel, through which air flows generating a great deal of wind power, the channel of friendship strengthens the heart, contributes to the focusing of the mind, and reaches out into the lives of others, regardless of whether we approve or disapprove of them. Such communications express a noble way of life.

A fearless element permeates authentic loving kindness, and it is clear that the power of such love is stronger than any destructive force. There is an old Buddhist story that is much appreciated by monks. Several centuries ago, at the gates of the monastery, the abbot greeted a warlord whose tyranny terrified the local people of the region. The abbot bowed to him. The warlord, with his huge sword raised high, said to the abbot, "I am the general that can chop you in half without blinking an eyelid." The abbot bowed again before the warlord and replied, "I am the Buddhist monk that can be chopped in half without blinking an eyelid."

We can begin to experience within ourselves that the power of friendship can run deep into our being, providing us with a source of energy and keeping us firm and steady at any time. Under the influence of negativity, agitation, and cynicism, it may be hard for us to deal wisely with the difficult states of mind of others. Rumi, the thirteenth-century poet from Balkh, Afghanistan, said we should regard all states of mind as guests visiting our inner life.

THE GUEST HOUSE

This being human is a guest house
Every morning a new arrival.
A joy, a depression, a meanness
Some momentary awareness comes
As an unexpected visitor
Welcome and entertain them all![3]

Regular deep friendship meditations, including welcoming as
guests our various states of mind, belong to the practice of
transforming the inner life.

Despite facing huge difficulties, there are some beautiful human
beings who express a depth of friendship and tolerance that we
applaud. Such people live a gracious and sensitive existence, even
when others treat them badly. They have a power that endeavors
to express something deep and significant, an act of purity, a
demonstration of a warm heart that reaches out to others, even
those who do not know how to reciprocate in the same way. We have much to learn
from such people, through their presence in our lives or through what they have
written. We need every human resource possible in this world to cultivate this power
of friendship, of deep loving kindness, that transforms our own lives and the lives of
others. When we take all of this into genuine consideration, it becomes obvious why
the Buddha said that the whole of the spiritual life is lived for such friendship.

We need to apply the practice of loving kindness so that it influences everything that
we do and all those we contact. It is these gestures that genuinely make a difference
to our world. The short-lived happiness we experience through entertainment, sport,
and consumer culture is not what people are crying out for. It is love. It is deep
friendship. It is direct expressions of kindness. It is a person-to-person thing, a
communication that endeavors to uplift the spirit, understand the problem, and
inspire vision.

Genuine love manifests in different expressions, such as friendship, compassion, kindness, gratitude, appreciation, generosity, and humility. Such love expresses itself freely, not defined through various conditions, not offered in exchange for something, but revealed as an offering to life. There is a wholeness to this love—it never creates divisions of "for" and "against," but seeks to express a unitive sense of things. Such love embraces the majestic sweep of existence without neglecting the ordinary and the everyday. The unstoppable force of friendship marks the sign of a mature and evolved human being.

EXERCISE: WRITING A PRAYER OF FRIENDSHIP

Write out a Prayer of Friendship and read it as a meditation on a regular basis. Here is an example:

May my mother and father live in peace and harmony.

May my brothers and sisters live in peace and harmony.

May my friends and neighbors live in peace and harmony.

May the friendly, strangers, and the unfriendly live in peace and harmony.

May I live in peace and harmony.

May my words and actions contribute to the happiness and welfare of others.

May the power of my friendship transform difficult situations.

May all beings live in peace and harmony.

EXERCISE: EXPRESSING FRIENDSHIP

Practice to express gestures of friendship on a daily basis.

At times, observe noble silence rather than engage in negative reactivity.

Listen to the kind voice within rather than the hard and harsh one.

Wait at least 24 hours before mailing a letter or sending an e-mail that reveals anger.

Develop a warmth and generosity of spirit rather than remaining stuck in old patterns.

Remember to treat others as you wish to be treated.

empowering patience

Patience is the capacity to stay steady, despite information that gives uncertainty to an outcome. Through mindfulness practice here and now, we learn to stay grounded in both the short and long term. Without patience, we become adversely affected by what we hear, sense, or think. We find levels of agitation increasing through the desire for something to change more quickly than the circumstances allow.

Impatience

There are countless situations in which we may lose our patience. We might find ourselves waiting:

- *for the outcome of medical tests*
- *for a conflicting situation to be resolved*
- *to meet somebody when we are not sure if they will remember the appointment*
- *for an important telephone call*
- *for somebody to complete a task that they have agreed to do*
- *for our teenage daughter to return home from a party*

If we observe our impatience, we will notice the rising tension in the body, the welling up of unpleasant emotions, and a sequence of thoughts that fans the fire of our tensions and feelings. Others may end up having to deal with our agitation or wrath, even though it has nothing to do with them. We might need to ask ourselves why we allow ourselves to behave in this way. Impatience can intensify until we become intolerant, burning up inner contentment and appreciation for people and situations. The Buddha said that we can do more harm to ourselves than our worst enemy can.

If we become truly mindful of the impact of this state of mind, it will lead to inner change, and to an understanding that life has its own movement, free from slavery to our demands. Not suprisingly, the Buddha listed patience as the highest quality of mind, since it allows us the opportunity to acknowledge inner peace in the face of the unexpected and unknown. When the flow of life runs according to our wishes, uninterrupted by difficult information or concerns, the significance of patience seems a minor consideration. All that can change rather quickly with a single thought, fear, conversation, or letter.

Our calm and peaceful inner world can be suddenly shattered when the forces of impatience begin mobilizing themselves from within. We want others or ourselves to conform to expectations, although in many situations the resolution of an issue may be out of everybody's hands. When we feel impatient, we are vulnerable to other states of mind. Worry, anxiety, agitation, and anger become unwelcome bedfellows to our unsettled mind, and we cling to the subject-matter or issue that is concerning us. There seems no way out at the time. Impatience gets a grip on our consciousness, pushing and pulling our mind around as though the only thing that matters in the world is the resolution of an unsettled and indeterminate issue.

Patience is a spiritual practice that works to transform our relationship to uncertain situations that we face. We can cultivate patience, whether we are waiting for the kettle to boil, or for the postal carrier to deliver an important letter. Mindfully breathing through our waves of impatience, we connect and reconnect with each moment to cool out the rising heat in the mind, if not in the body as well.

We have all had the experience of impatience when we are traveling, often when waiting for a delayed train or flight. We complain bitterly, barge past others, and harass staff, who are often powerless to change the situation. Are we like this in other areas of life, too? It takes self-honesty to admit that our abrasive manner says more about ourselves than about the situation we are in. Awareness of reality and the humility to recognize that we cannot control circumstances serve as vehicles to develop a mature response to situations. When we are impatient, we may succeed in getting our own way, but others will resent our obnoxious manner.

Buddhists monks and nuns use the seasons as a reminder of the importance of patience, recognizing in the turning of the year that the seasons unfold in their own time and that there is a time and place for everything. We can practice staying with that unfoldment rather than trying to leap ahead of current events. One of the most widely quoted Buddhist comments on this attunement to natural unfoldment is: "Spring comes, green grass grows by itself." We should contemplate this, and let the truth of this simple statement travel deep within—it will act like a good friend in testing times.

For anything to arise in this world, there is a simple prerequisite: the necessary conditions must be present. We can easily forget this, and start imagining that just because we want something it should take place. Impatience can be the undoing of an intelligent mind, inner peace, and a realistic approach to the reality of events. If we work to develop patience, we will discover fresh ways to work with situations without becoming either angry about or submissive to unexpected circumstances.

It ought to be clear to us that there is a close relationship between love and patience. For example, in a close friendship there is a wealth of kindness and appreciation that flows between two people. Values such as punctuality don't seem to matter too much. Love provides a degree of tolerance and acceptance of the other person. However, as time passes, expectations can unconsciously begin to build up. The difference between the punctual and the less than punctual may develop until it gives rise to a demand born of impatience. As the demands increase, the love diminishes. Time-keeping becomes a point of irritation, which leads to a full-blown argument. One person expects the other to be punctual, while the other expects his or her friend to be flexible and generous about it. Sometimes this is due to differences in culture or priorities.

Spiritual Practice

Patience is a beautiful quality of mind that we need to cultivate and develop as a primary spiritual practice. It provides a way of learning to love life as it unfolds, free from the demands of the mind seeking order, time, and the imposition of fixed ideas of how things should be. Stepping outside this enclosed and restricted circle of the mind, we experience a natural, organic patience that finds itself in tune with the flow of life, regardless of whether it serves our needs.

In this sublime attunement to things, we feel at peace with whatever is happening. A free mind carries notions of time and other mental constructions very lightly, since they are frequently out of touch with the immediacy of things. There is a wonder to be discovered in the midst of confusion and chaos that reflects the flow of events that no individual can fix. Life is never a mechanical and orderly event, but the interplay of a myriad conditions forming and dissolving together moment after moment. It is a wondrous thing.

EXERCISE: DEVELOPING PATIENCE

Impatience easily shows itself in tone of voice, attitude, and body language.
Use breathing exercises (as mentioned in the opening chapter) to allow the cells to relax.
Remind yourself that your practice is to develop patience. Acknowledge that you will experience setbacks. Keep practicing patience for your own peace of mind as well as to take the pressure off others.

EXERCISE: MAINTAINING PATIENCE

Write out a list of the benefits of patience.
Reflect on the list and memorize two or three points. Endeavor to remember them even in moments of brief impatience.
Acknowledge that calmness is far preferable to being uptight when events do not go your way.
Develop steadfastness in the here and now through acceptance, rather than developing intolerance.

practicing meditation

The importance and value of meditation in our daily lives cannot be emphasized enough. It is an essential feature of living with wisdom and understanding. Meditation gives access to a depth within ourselves that moves consciousness beyond its usual confined and limited perceptions. For countless generations enlightened teachers have endorsed meditation as an indispensable feature of the spiritual life.

Theories of evolution emphasize the development of the human species through the selection of certain characteristics, and involve the comparison of the present with the past. It is not so easy to determine whether human beings have evolved inwardly in terms of our relationship with each other and with the Earth itself. Greed, hate, and delusion, the three "poisons of the mind" in the Buddhist tradition, have been for

a long time the curse of the Earth. Selfish and brutal desire has troubled humankind and caused untold damage to others and our natural resources. We have waged war upon each other and the Earth. Have we really evolved wisely as a species over the past few thousand years? Meditation is directly concerned with the inner evolution of consciousness and the inner transformation of a person, so that an intelligent and thoughtful approach to life is at the foreground of human existence.

Meditation contributes to the healing of inner wounds, and cultivates equanimity and inner peace. Developing such practices, we also generate appropriate conditions for realizations about the nature of existence, unavailable through thoughts and intellectual activity. If we develop meditation practice, as well as bringing mindfulness and insight to the fullness of the day, we have the potential to live a truly awakened life rather than drifting or hurrying from one day to the next.

What is meant by meditation? There are four primary ways of regarding meditation. Each one is valid.

MEDITATION: MEANINGS AND METHODS

1 Meditation means simply "observation," "mindfulness," "awareness," "being conscious," "receptivity," and "paying attention to." It is when we apply these principles at the moment-to-moment level that we speak of it as the experience of meditation. We can experience meditation in the formal posture such as sitting cross-legged or with a straight back in a chair or giving moment-to-moment attention to an activity.

2 Meditation is regarded as a prescription. This kind of meditation adheres strictly to method and technique to enhance concentration and discipline, especially in the formal sitting posture (on a chair or cross-legged) with a straight back and one hand resting on the other in the lap. The meditator applies the method or technique once or twice a day, from 15 minutes to up to an hour, to develop calm and clarity.

3 A state of meditation arises spontaneously. A quietude of feelings, stillness, and a sense of harmony with the world around is experienced. Thoughts fade away, the brain cells become quiet and there is a sense of inner well-being. In this meditative space, the elements of stillness and silence become predominant. There is a palpable sense of the extraordinary presence of life without any division or fragmentation.

4 Meditation is a rare mystical state that transcends the conventional world. Some associate meditation with the ultimate state of consciousness. The implication of this is that few actually reach this state of meditation. To be in a state of meditation is to be with God. To be with God is to abide in meditation. In the nondualistic tradition of India, the word for this meditation is Samadhi. Samadhi remains forever established, whether we exist or not.

There is a certain kind of process that takes place when we meditate that contributes to a state of inner restfulness. There is something beautiful about such contentment, whether we are sitting still or moving. There is no pressure in the mind, no desire to pursue anything or to achieve anything. There are no demands on ourselves or on others. Our life then participates in the fullness of things. Such meditation is a state of clear abiding.

Types of Meditation

Whether our meditation is in the form of sustainable mindfulness during the day, the formal application of method and technique, or the spontaneous states of meditation, by practicing we will experience a noticeable and self-evident increase in healthy qualities of mind, and a diminishing of unhealthy states. There will be a clear change in our relationship to life. We experience this within ourselves, and others may see that we have changed, too. These changes reveal themselves in two tangible ways. There is greater calmness in our life and more insight as well. The Buddha pointed to this realization through a remarkable analogy. He tells us to consider our body as a castle, with the five sense doors functioning as windows in the castle. Acting as messengers, two birds fly through the windows of the castle bringing in a message to the lord of the castle, whose name is Mindfulness. The names of the messengers are Calm and Insight. They bring the message of liberation to the lord of the castle.

It is important to understand that there are different viewpoints within the different meditation traditions. Some meditation teachers express concern about restricting meditation to a formal posture at specific times of the day. They feel that this isolates meditation from the totality of the day. They encourage us to bring a meditative focus to every single activity, no matter what it is. If we only use formal meditation, there is a danger of concluding that our practice and inner work only really matter during those times at the expense and neglect of the rest of the day.

Other meditation teachers take a different view. They insist on regular, formal meditation, advocating that we devote as much as one hour in the morning and another hour in the evening to formal meditation to keep the mind focused, concentrated, and clear. These teachers feel that neglect of formal meditation means that we easily drift along. We believe in the power of daily mindfulness, but we deceive ourselves because the power of mind and concentrated presence is not accessible. Advocates of these traditions emphasize the importance of the discipline of formal meditation.

There are other meditation teachers who challenge both of these views. They claim that both formal meditation and mindfulness in daily life require a lot of effort. This effort is an expression of spiritual desire, a subtle form of egotism, to achieve a desired end. The effort to be mindful exposes a desire to have control over the inner life, as well as over events around us. These teachers say that meditation arises spontaneously. There is nothing that we can do. We should treat, they say, any effort as a distraction, a resistance to experiencing meditation and realization.

We have to decide through our own experience rather than letting one tradition of meditation or another determine our views. From my experience, I believe it is invaluable to explore strict meditation practices, to apply mindfulness to daily life, and to be receptive to a meditative state of being that arises spontaneously. We do not have to adopt an exclusive or narrow view of the process of meditation.

I have come across the extraordinary benefits of meditation in the formal posture many times, even when it is not specifically clear to the person meditating what the benefits are! Appreciation of the benefits often arises outside the posture rather than within. It is not always easy to see the correlation. One meditator told me that she never seemed able to concentrate on two successive breaths in meditation before her mind wandered, yet she felt an enormous change for the better taking place in her life. Sometimes changes take place beneath the conscious level.

Many practitioners of meditation say they struggle at times to bring their attention to the breathing or to the here and now. It seems that throughout the entire duration of the practice, the mind acts like a wild monkey, jumping backward and forward from one thing to another, with little opportunity to anchor itself in the present moment or a specific feature of it. This becomes frustrating when we feel the hopelessness of trying to remain calm and steady in the here and now. At times, consciousness remains doggedly determined to be anywhere but in the present. It is frequently common to hear of the uphill task that many experience in getting their mind to cooperate with as simple an instruction as "watch the breath" or "be here and now." We experience the mind as unruly, undisciplined, and fragmented, and as recalcitrant as an angry teenager. Refusing to stay settled in the moment, the mind leaps about from one thing to another. Meditation shakes us up a great deal when we see how little real control we have over the mind, no matter how much the ego tells us that we have our life really together.

EXERCISES: FURTHERING MEDITATION PRACTICE

1 Participate in a retreat, workshop, or meditation class under the guidance and instruction of a dedicated meditation teacher. As with any spiritual discipline, there are many questions that can arise, the answers to which cannot always be found in books. There is no substitute for direct communication with a teacher who is further along the spiritual path. A meditation teacher may belong to a particular tradition—try to see what is relevant for your spiritual practice through your own experience. You do not have to take on board the whole package, or identify with a tradition unless it feels very comfortable.

2 Practice formal meditation. The amount of time that you sit and meditate is as important as the regular application of meditation. If you can meditate at home three or four times a week for twenty minutes at a time, it will enhance your practice a great deal. It will take a quiet determination to get into the general rhythm of regular meditation. Some people give their daily meditation practice their highest priority, meditating morning and evening for up to one hour each session.

3 Practice meditation as moment-to-moment attention during the course of the day. This means applying meditative presence to every activity, such as when washing the dishes. Often, we would rather get on with something else, since we perceive such mundane household tasks as chores rather than opportunities for meditation practice. These familiar tasks deserve our calm attention. We wash the dishes in order to experience washing the dishes. The two major sense doors at work are the eyes and the hands. We engage in giving a conscious presence to the task, right through from beginning to the end. The same principle applies to every task and activity, whether sitting down in a chair, expressing some form of movement, or listening to another. There is a conscious sense of being present, of abiding mindfully and peacefully, here and now. Such meditative mindfulness helps to cut wasted energy through unnecessary use of the body and supports a sense of harmony of body with mind and mind with body.

Witnessing

The various features of meditation also help us to develop the ability to witness. Witnessing has the primary role in daily life of keeping our minds steady and clear so that we avoid being completely subject to events, both inner and outer, that push or pull our thoughts in one direction or another. Witnessing is not a way to avoid feelings or emotions. It is quite the contrary. It is a way to see them clearly so that we develop the skill to respond wisely to our emotional life. If the hand is too close to our face, we cannot see the line of the hand clearly. There are occasions in daily life when we easily slip into taking sides. We think we always know what is right or wrong, good or evil, better or worse, but sometimes we choose a side too quickly. Witnessing is about stopping to question, about examining all angles before adopting a position.

Meditation gives support to the inner witness so that we examine both sides of a situation impartially to find out whether there is an alternative way of looking at it. From the standpoint of the witness, the position of for and against says little about the issue and more about the attitude.

The power of the witness generates space that enables us to realize a more thoughtful and wise view of events, instead of submitting to the initial impulse to take sides. Applying these basic principles of the witness, we move closer to an undivided sense of life. This intimacy with existence enables us to engage creatively and fully with the various tasks at hand. The inner life develops a sublime strength through attending to the various circumstances in our life arising from within or without. Through such a meditative awareness we are knocking on the door of inner freedom of being, no matter where we are.

EXERCISE: APPLYING MEDITATION TO YOUR LIFE

Try to attend a retreat, a workshop, or a class on meditation with a meditation teacher.
Make time every week for formal meditation. Use guided meditations.
Sit in the formal posture with a straight back, either cross-legged, kneeling using a wooden stool, or in an upright chair. Meditate to be present here and now.
Write out some lines of meaningful poetry, uplifting spiritual insights, or readings from sacred texts. Read slowly and mindfully to absorb the wisdom. Use the formal posture mentioned above.
Bring meditation into your daily life as an invaluable resource.

EXERCISES: APPLYING MINDFULNESS TO EVERYDAY ACTIVITIES

Make certain tasks mindfulness meditations, whether washing the dishes, gardening, making a cup of tea, or walking along the street.
Practice to be truly conscious of every expression of the task.
Meditation is applying mindfulness without feelings of being hurried or under pressure.
Develop moment-to-moment attention with the ordinary and everyday so
· that there is a deep and abiding interest in living a more conscious existence.

LIVING WITH WISDOM AND COMPASSION

Information, Knowledge, and Wisdom

A saintly Buddhist monk and Cambodian Patriarch, the Venerable Maha Ghosananda, who has been nominated for the Nobel Peace Prize on four occasions, often reminds people of a simple truth he realized when he says to them:

The thought manifests as the word.
The word manifests as the deed.
The deed develops into the habit.
The habit hardens into the character.
The character gives birth to the destiny.
So, watch your thoughts with care.
And let them spring from love
Born out of respect for all beings.

We have become so infatuated with our thoughts, especially our memories and our plans, that we barely have enough mindfulness left to take an honest look at the present moment. There is no ultimate satisfaction in this way of living since it is images, projections, and stories that make up our reality. Part of mindfulness practice consists of going beyond these stories about ourselves, of who we think we are, to get in touch with the real world and the intimacy of our relationship with it here and now.

We often talk about yesterday or tomorrow as if it all has some substantial significance. Instead, we need to remember that the "past" and "future" emerge as thoughts out of the here and now. No matter how much we speak about the past or the future, whether yesterday or tomorrow, millions of years ago, or millions of years in the future, our views and opinions emerge out of the conditions of our mind in the present moment. Yet, we rarely seem to take full note of this fact. Outside the conviction of the mind, there is no "past" or "future." Only human beings construct yesterday or tomorrow. Mindfulness practice grounds us in the immediate reality. Then we can see the world afresh, rather than being bound up with beliefs and projections constructed around time. To see the world afresh generates wisdom and compassion naturally.

It is important to distinguish between information, knowledge, and wisdom. Today we have access to a great deal of information, which we find in newspapers, books, television programs, libraries, and, of course, the Internet. We could not possibly digest the staggering amount of information available to us. When we reflect on or adopt views on the information we have, we gain knowledge. We may then speak or write about the subject, or we might display our knowledge through particular skills, such as repairing a car, engaging in home improvement tasks, or creating something.

Knowledge about something also has to translate itself into wisdom. The process of conversion from knowledge to wisdom may take time, or insights may come dramatically. It is never enough just to talk about things. Knowledge needs the support of two other factors: intention to change and insight into what is going on. Without intention and insight, we struggle along, gaining a superficial level of knowledge about our problems, but that knowledge lacks the power to change them. We need a depth of inner listening to dig out the wisdom.

Similarly, we may be troubled by a situation of conflict we are in with another person, and our heart and mind may find it hard to settle down. We dwell on our fears, anger, and vulnerability to rejection, and experience more discontent. To be wise in such a situation requires intentional cultivation of calmness, the quiet resolution not to inflame our emotions, and the capacity to take appropriate steps to resolve the problem. Mindfulness training, meditation, and inquiry give priority to insight at the time of the issue rather than relying on hindsight.

Perhaps we have been diagnosed with an illness. Some of us have complete confidence in our physicians and rely on them completely, taking their advice and following their prescriptions. Others of us may adopt a different approach, pursuing information, searching through the Internet and textbooks, and consulting with others. Referring to the powers of mind, the Buddha said trust and wisdom complement each other. Through an excess of faith, we can rely too much on others, thus prohibiting the opportunity to find out for ourselves what would be appropriate. However, too much knowledge can lead to doubts and confusion as we find different conclusions from varying sources. We can become infatuated with the endless pursuit of information and accumulate much knowledge, yet we still have to find wisdom and balance it with trust to deal with our situation. We need to apply wisdom to our emotional, intellectual, and physical life so that we can abide clearly, purposefully, and at peace with a situation.

How do we know when we are making the shift from knowledge to wisdom? Wisdom shows itself tangibly as a change in thinking that has a calming influence on the emotions. There is a dissipation of anxiety and fearful projections into the future, and a greater capacity to live one day at a time rather than with anguish and painful thoughts rolling around in our heads as we struggle to make sense of what is going on. When knowledge has undergone some genuine change, we actually think about things differently, and, most importantly of all, we feel differently about them as well. This is the sign of conversion from knowledge to wisdom.

Practicing Compassion

It is not unusual to believe that compassion is something that we have or don't have. Wisdom encourages us to develop and apply compassion since it expresses wisdom about our relationship to the world. Meditation on kindness and friendship toward others acts as an important stepping stone on the path to compassion.

Some people in secular culture express a wise approach to daily life through their capacity to let go of issues, to regard them as a challenge, and to live with passion. A spiritual approach to life goes further than this. It points to an ultimate freedom through developing a deeply caring relationship with every area of existence.

Meditation, reflection, communication with others, acts of selfless service, and wise use of resources are steps along the path to a noble way of living. It is an enormous challenge to adopt a compassionate view toward all forms of life on Earth. If we are not charged up with ambition, the desire to make a name for ourselves, or the need to become rich, we can live a life

of service from one day to the next. Compassion toward others is an indispensable feature of mindful living.

We can make a meaningful contribution to the welfare of people, animals, and the environment. Compassion is wisdom that directly benefits others. For generations, Buddhists have illustrated this with the image of a great bird flying through the air—one wing is for compassion and the other wing is for wisdom. If we apply both wings to our journey through existence, we abide in a meaningful and balanced way.

If we put our hearts into mindful living, our hearts will make demands of us. We will then explore the real significance of existence and find that all events, situations, and people are connected. In some extraordinary way, what we do for some people we are doing for everyone. In the spirit of the teachings and practices outlined in this book, we will place wisdom and compassion at the center of our existence and be on the road to leading a truly fulfilled and enlightened life.

EXERCISE: STRIVING FOR WISDOM

Examine your relationship to information, knowledge, and wisdom.

Practice using discernment with regard to information.

Make every effort to find out what is a wise action or a wise response
to a situation.

Listen to that response and make a determination to apply it.

Give more priority to wisdom over information and knowledge.

EXERCISE: EXPLORING INTERCONNECTION WITH OTHERS

Examine your commitment to serve others.

What practical steps can you take to support the needs of others?

Reflect on the difference between expressing love and compassion and
holding onto notions of doing good.

If you are reasonably free from anguish and pain, then explore ways to share
your freedom with others, near or far.

Remember the great depth of interconnection we have with each other.

May all beings live in peace.
May all beings live in harmony.
May all beings live a free and enlightened life.

Further Reading – Other Books by Christopher Titmuss

An Awakened Life: Uncommon Wisdom from Everyday Experience
Published by Rider Books, UK (1999); Shambhala Publications, USA (2000).

Buddhist Wisdom for Daily Living
Published by Godsfield Press, UK; Walking Stick Press, USA (2001).

Light on Enlightenment: Revolutionary Teachings of the Inner Life
Published by Rider Books, UK (1998); Shambhala Publications, USA (1999).

The Little Box of Inner Calm
Packaged by Quarto Press, London. Published by Barron's Educational Series, Inc., USA (1999).

Spirit of Change: Voices of Hope for a Better World
Published by Greenprint, UK (1990); Hunter House, USA (1993).

The Buddha's Book of Daily Meditations: A Year of Wisdom, Compassion, and Happiness
Published by Rider Books, UK (2001); Three Rivers Press, USA (2001).

The Profound and the Profane: An Inquiry into Spiritual Awakening
Published by Insight Books, Totnes, UK (1993); distributed by Wisdom Books, UK; Buddhist Publishing Group, USA (1993).

Transforming our Terror: A Spiritual Approach to Making Sense of Senseless Tragedy
Published by Godsfield Press, UK (2002); Barron's Educational Series, Inc., USA (2002).

All above books are available from:
Insight Books (Totnes), c/o Gaia House, West Ogwell, near Newton Abbot, Devon TQ12, UK.
Tel: +44 (0)1626 333613
Fax: +44 (0)1626 352 650
E-mail: generalinquiries@gaiahouse.co.uk
Websites: http://www.gaiahouse.co.uk,
http://www.insightmeditation.org,
http://www.dharmanetwork.org.
(Please add £2.00 for each book for post and package for overseas mailing.)

Notes

[1] Page 59 *Full Catastrophe Living*, Jon Kabat-Zinn, published by Bantam Doubleday Publishing Group, USA (1990)

[2] Page 77 quote from *The Prophet*, Kahil Gibran, published by Senate Press Ltd, UK (1997).

[3] Page 106 quote from *The Essential Rumi*, translated by Coleman Barks, published by Harper Collins, USA (1995).

Author Acknowledgments

During the 1970s I spent six years as a Buddhist monk in Thailand and India where I learned about and practiced the great importance of mindfulness and insight meditation as a deep spiritual practice for an enlightened life. I am very grateful to have had the opportunity for sustained contact with the Buddhist tradition and its ongoing exploration of the human condition.

I wish to thank Godsfield Press in Great Britain for publishing this book and the editors, designers, picture researchers, and layout artists at The Bridgewater Book Company for all their efforts in putting this book together. I wish to express particular appreciation to Mark Truman, Sarah Howerd, Nicola Wright, and Lisa McCormick for their care and precision in the project.

Special thanks to Nshorna Titmuss, my daughter, for kindly transcribing much of the material in this book.

Picture Acknowledgments

Corbis: pp 8b, 11, 12, 14b, 23, 30, 38, 39, 42, 48, 49, 51, 53, 66, 67, 80, 89, 94, 99, 101, 103, 116, 120, 121, 123, 124; GettyOneStone: pp 9, 13, 15, 17, 33, 35, 57, 71, 85, 88, 102, 108, 112, 114, 117, 118; Image Bank: pp 27, 34b, 44b, 54, 60, 63, 66c, 69, 79, 96, 110; Telegraph Colour Library: pp 20, 77, 105.

INDEX